Is Bipartisanship Dead?

A Report from the Senate

Is Bipartisanship Dead?
A Report from the Senate

Ross K. Baker

Paradigm Publishers
Boulder • London

Copyright © 2015 Paradigm Publishers

Published in the United States by Paradigm Publishers, 5589 Arapahoe Avenue, Boulder, CO 80303 USA.

Paradigm Publishers is the trade name of Birkenkamp & Company, LLC, Dean Birkenkamp, President and Publisher.

Library of Congress Cataloging-in-Publication Data

Baker, Ross K.
  Is bipartisanship dead? : a report from the Senate / Ross K. Baker.
     pages cm.
  Includes bibliographical references and index.
  ISBN 978-1-61205-421-6 (hardcover : alk. paper) —
ISBN 978-1-61205-824-5 (library ebook) — ISBN 978-1-61205-422-3
(pbk. : alk. paper) — ISBN 978-1-61205-825-2 (consumer ebook)
  1. United States. Congress. Senate. 2. United States. Congress.
Senate—Leadership. 3. United States. Congress. Senate—Committees.
4. Political culture—United States. 5. Political parties—United States.
6. Political leadership—United States.
7. Legislative power—United States. I. Title.
  JK1161.B345 2015
  328.73'071—dc23
                                                            2014026635

Printed and bound in the United States of America on acid-free paper that meets the standards of the American National Standard for Permanence of Paper for Printed Library Materials.

Designed and Typeset by Straight Creek Bookmakers.

19 18 17 16 15 1 2 3 4 5

To my dear Millennials, who, in time, will sort things out.

Molly, Ben, and Elizabeth

Jack and Maddie

CONTENTS

ACKNOWLEDGMENTS

In 2008 and 2012, while on sabbatical leave from Rutgers University, I was hosted in Washington by the majority leader of the United States Senate. My residency on his staff gave me an unparalleled perspective that I could not have gained in the offices of any of the ninety-nine other senators. The view from room S-221 of the Capitol looked out on not only the grandeur of the National Mall, but on the entirety of what has been characterized, perhaps too generously, as "the world's greatest deliberative body."

My first landing on "Planet Reid" was a lunch at a restaurant in Washington's Union Station to discuss the terms of my residency. It was there that I met for the first time the man who would ease my way into the leader's office, but also serve as my guide and support through my two sabbaticals: deputy chief of staff David McCallum.

David may have been the first, but was certainly not the only member of the Reid staff to make me feel at home and to interpret for me the mysterious folkways of the Senate—arcane rituals that I though I knew all about as a scholar specializing in the institution.

Let me acknowledge some of them—with apologies, in advance, for those I might have overlooked. At the top of the list is the legendary Bill Dauster, Senator Reid's other deputy chief of staff, whose broad intellectual reach would grace the faculty of any great university. Kindly in manner and accessible even at the busiest of times, his learned perspective belies the common perception of Hill staffers as dreary policy wonks.

My roommate in my Capitol offices on both Senate sojourns was Carolyn Gluck, Senator Reid's senior expert on women's issues. The title "senior" doesn't sit very well on Carolyn, whose youthful enthusiasm and boundless energy, which enable her to do her job so effectively and raise two children, make an admirable example of the working mom.

The top staff guy in Reid's office is David Krone, who assumed the post just before I arrived in 2012. He gave me access that I had no reason to expect from someone so deeply engaged in the strategizing and maneuvering associated with the politics of the Senate. He never exhibited the slightest irritation at questions I posed to him that he can only have thought were quite naive.

The senior policy experts in the leadership office are the leader's emissaries to the committees of the Senate. They bring the leader up to date on what is going on in the committees for which they are responsible, and they are his intelligence network. Those most helpful to me were Bruce King, whose specialty is the metaphysical world of the federal budget; Jessica Lewis, who is the resident foreign-policy expert; Serena Hoy, who is the leader's liaison to the Judiciary Committee; Bob Greenawalt, who covers the Finance Committee; Kasey Gillette on Agriculture; Tommy Ross, the senator's expert on national security; and Gavin Parke, who works with the Committee on Homeland Security and Governmental Affairs.

I want to thank my old friend and mentor (although he is younger than I am) Bert Carp, who adds integrity to the much-maligned profession of lobbying and who provided the title for this book. I am also grateful to the historian of the US Senate, Don Ritchie, whose knowledge of the institution is incomparable; and to Nancy Kervin, of the Senate Library, who knows everything that's ever been written about the Senate and is happy to track it down.

In the final stages of the book, Candace Cunningham, my editor, rode out of the West to flag my gaffes and errors and to make the book as technically accurate as possible. Her good humor and willingness to track down missing URLs and repair botched endnotes made her indispensable at a critical time.

Finally, but by no means last in my thoughts, is my wife Ellen Hulme—who suffered through my absences in the two periods I was in Washington. I'm happy I fell in love with a woman who could tolerate long deployments.

Introduction

In the United States Senate, sorting out what is partisan and what is bipartisan is no simple task. For example, bills and amendments that are introduced by a Democrat and a Republican—a very common event in the Senate—can, as they pass through the legislative process, increasingly bear the imprint of only one party. The legislative process is one in which there are many veto points and in which its "regular order" is preempted by the intervention of party leaders. Such measures may produce, in their ultimate stages, a starkly polarized vote despite the fact that they were encoded with bipartisan DNA earlier in the process.

Let's cite a recent example—the 2009 Patient Protection and Affordable Care Act, which came to be known as "Obamacare," first by its detractors and subsequently by President Obama himself. Throughout this book, reference will be made to Obamacare and to the final vote in both houses, in which not a single Republican vote was recorded in its favor. Yet, when we examine what the bill contained and what it did not contain, it is clear that important concessions were made, early in the process, in the hope that bipartisan support could be secured.

Certainly, the absence of what was called the "public option" tells us that this particular provision, which would have established a publicly run health insurance program alongside the private plans, was dropped in the hope of attracting Republicans (and an influential independent, Connecticut's Joseph Lieberman). Had these concessions not been made and had the vote not gone as it did, it would be fair to say that Obamacare was a purely partisan enterprise. But it was marked by its origins as a bill that, while still in the Finance Committee, had the possibility of Republican support had other events not intervened.

Polarization, moreover, is far easier to document than bipartisanship because it is less elusive. The compilation and analysis of roll-call votes is unequivocal in painting a picture, over time, of hardened lines of battle between Democrats and Republicans.[1]

Those seeking examples of bipartisanship in the Senate labor under a burden: some bipartisanship occurs in plain view; other expressions of it fly beneath the radar of the media and academic researchers. Furthermore, because only a modest amount of this bipartisanship shows up as important legislation signed into law, it encounters the charge that it amounts to nothing more than an empty ritual of civility or the kind of reassuring happy-talk that might be expected from members of an institution suffering from low approval ratings.

Throughout the book, we will see examples of substantial bipartisan cooperation at the stage of the legislative process that takes place in the committees of the Senate and that even have Democrats and Republicans joining forces and going on record with their votes to report out a bill. Often, however, the bipartisan product is rejected or mutilated in the more combative environment of the Senate floor, where the role of party leaders, and the caucuses they represent, become more influential.

It would be too extreme a statement to say that there is natural hostility to bipartisan legislation on the part of party leaders. But the forces that drive party leaders to defend the seats of fellow partisans and, if possible, expand their numbers, are often at odds with measures that have support from senators of the rival party. Inasmuch as one of the responsibilities of a party leader in the Senate is to rally the more ideologically committed members of the party base, a bill that seems to give away too much to the other side may be scuttled by a party leader. Sometimes, it is just that party leaders don't want an opposition senator to look good, especially if that person is up for reelection.

This wariness of bipartisanship by party leaders is a product of a number of factors, one of which has been called the "permanent campaign,"[2] in which legislative goals are subordinated to "messaging" bills and amendments that promote the political goals of one's own party and demean those of the opposition. These are measures that no one expects will pass but are introduced purely for their power to do political mischief. Also, control of the Senate has been a close-run thing in recent years, giving rise to the faux legislation of messaging.

Congressional scholar Frances Lee has argued that it is the regular transfer of power over the past three decades from Democrats to Republicans and back again that has put the Senate on a kind of war footing, with both sides "staging votes for the precise purpose of ensuring that the parties will vote on opposite sides."[3] Lee goes on to suggest that these votes, calculated to embarrass opponents and rally a party base, may be less reflective of real polarization and instead are an artifact of how the permanent campaign plays out on the floor of the Senate.

It is worth noting that when the question "Is bipartisanship dead?" was posed to a dozen senators—six Democrats and six Republicans—the answer was uniformly "No." Having posed the question in a neutral fashion and avoided the appearance of being a cheerleader for bipartisanship, I had to conclude that beneath the strident messaging and polarized roll-call votes, something subtle but important is going on in the Senate that may require us to reexamine the meaning of bipartisanship.

It is the goal of this book to look critically at bipartisanship in the Senate and come to some conclusions about the various manifestations of bipartisanship in the chamber, if indeed such exist. It may require us to "define down" the term in a way that may not be very satisfying, insofar as it embraces conduct that not everyone would consider significant in public policy terms. Yet such examples may have important institutional implications for the Senate.

I will try to not overvalue bipartisanship and will question its genuineness even in those cases in which it would appear to all the world to be present. And I will not treat bipartisanship as an end in itself, because there are enough instances of bipartisanship resulting in dubious public policy for us to not treat it as an absolute good. Nor will I conflate bipartisanship and simple civility. I will also not deny that real and enduring differences exist in the American public that inevitably limit the amount of bipartisanship that can be reasonably expected from those held accountable to such a divided citizenry.

I

BIPARTISANSHIP IN THE US SENATE

RECOVERY AND RELAPSE

One day in December 2012, the paradoxes of partisanship in the US Senate were on vivid display.

At 11:30 a.m., a press conference was held in the ornate anteroom of the old Senate Foreign Relations Committee hearing room on the first floor of the US Capitol Building for the purpose of raising support for the ratification by the Senate of the United Nations Convention on the Rights of Persons with Disabilities. Treaties, under the US Constitution, if they are to be binding on the United States, must be approved by a two-thirds vote of the Senate, or 67 senators.

Two of the American political world's most recognizable figures were sponsors of the treaty: Senator John Kerry, the Massachusetts Democrat who had been the Democratic presidential nominee in 2004 and subsequently nominated by President Obama for the post of secretary of state, and Senator

John McCain, an Arizona Republican who had been his party's unsuccessful presidential nominee in 2008.

Kerry and McCain shared a unique bond other than the fact that both had been nominated for the presidency and both had been defeated: both senators had served with distinction in the Vietnam War, although they emerged from it with clashing views about the rightness of the conflict. Kerry preceded McCain to the Senate by two years. For a time, the two new senators barely spoke a friendly word to each other. But as members of a congressional delegation on a fact-finding trip to the Middle East, the two men found themselves reminiscing about their wartime experiences on the lengthy plane trip and ended up leading the campaign to establish diplomatic relations with Vietnam.[1]

Kerry, as a member of the majority party, chairman of the Senate Foreign Relations Committee, and a co-sponsor with McCain of the treaty, spoke first. He was flanked by a dozen visibly disabled people, including a young former Army first lieutenant, Dan Berschinski, who stood behind Kerry, supported on his titanium prosthetic legs. Kerry (who, although nominated by President Obama as secretary of state, had yet to receive Senate confirmation) urged support of the treaty and yielded the lectern to McCain, who quipped facetiously, "Thank you, Mr. Secretary." After McCain's remarks, Kerry returned the wry compliment, saying "Thank you, Mr. President." At this point, Kerry reached around McCain, hugged him, and said, "This is what happens when you get losers up here."

The event was a pageant of bipartisan harmony. More than that, it was a display of one of the more notable relationships in the Senate and a signal to the nation and the world that, with the prestige of these two distinguished senators from different sides of the partisan aisle, the odds improved that the Senate would produce the votes required for ratification. Supporters of the treaty left little to chance. They reasoned that having a venerated Republican with some very special credentials speak on the subject of disability rights might swing some Republican senators toward support for ratification.

The Vote

The Democratic leader, Senator Harry Reid, had confidence that all the Democrats in his often-fractious caucus would vote to ratify the treaty. As of the conclusion of the senior staff meeting in Reid's office at 9:00 a.m. that morning, the count showed a solid 61 in favor of the treaty, including a handful of Republicans who were augmenting the 54 Democratic senators. What was in doubt was from where the other 6 votes would come.

The ratification vote, scheduled for noon, was preceded by the appearance in the chamber of one of the Senate's immortals: former Senator Robert Dole, the 89-year-old former Republican leader and 1996 Republican presidential nominee. A commanding figure in American politics for almost fifty years, Dole was now confined to a wheelchair and was pushed on to the Senate floor by an another Republican ex-senator, Dole's wife Elizabeth, who had represented North Carolina. Dole not only suffered from the ravages of age but also from the horrific battle wounds he had received in the fighting in northern Italy during World War II.[2]

But senators on the floor of the chamber that day required no outside prompting from an ex-colleague to remind them of the disabled currently among them. They needed only to glance across the chamber to the empty left sleeve of Senator Daniel Inouye, then the most senior member of the Senate and hence its president pro tem. Inouye was likewise a wounded veteran of the Italian campaign. There was also South Dakota's Tim Johnson, who moved in and out of the chamber in a motorized wheelchair as the result of a stroke, or even more conspicuously, John McCain, the cosponsor of the treaty, who was tortured as a prisoner of war in North Vietnam and is still unable to raise his arms above the level of his shoulders.

As the alphabetical roll call of the senators began, Paul Kane, congressional correspondent for the *Washington Post* tracked the vote. The vote cast by Senator Daniel Akaka, a Democrat from Hawaii, was an unsurprising aye. The next response stunned him. The name of Lamar Alexander, Republican of Tennessee, was called by the clerk, and he answered, "Nay." Kane turned to the reporter seated next to him and said, "This treaty is dead."[3]

Kane concluded that if a senator known for his moderation and internationalism was opposing the treaty, those less disposed to think well of the United Nations or, indeed, of treaties in general, would never contribute the six Republican votes required for ratification.

Described by a home-state newspaper as "a pragmatist who wants to undo the operational gridlock he sees in Washington [and who] ... resigned his post as Republican caucus chairman earlier this year to show himself independent of GOP leadership," Alexander had also become concerned that his soft-spoken conservatism might earn him a primary election challenger. Further, he worried that he, like other Senate moderate Republicans such as Robert Bennett of Utah and Richard Lugar of Indiana, who had been vanquished by ultra-conservative challengers, might be a marked man.[4]

The final vote was 61 ayes and 38 nays. One senator, Illinois Republican Mark Kirk, was recovering from a stroke and was not present to vote.

One curious fact about the vote was that the treaty had been previously approved and referred to the entire Senate by a bipartisan vote of 13–6 in the Foreign Relations Committee. Three Republicans on the committee—the ranking minority member, Richard G. Lugar of Indiana, plus Johnny Isakson of Georgia and John Barrasso of Wyoming—had supported reporting out the treaty, but on the ratification vote on December 4, 2012, one of the three, Senator Isakson, cast a vote against the treaty.

Senator Isakson's reason to vote to reject the treaty was the same as that of many Republican senators who had opposed it all along. Isakson explained,

> Basically, there were two schools of thought on opposition to the treaty. One was that we had no business doing it in a lame-duck session with twelve new members coming in in January; that it really ought to be done by the new Senate and not the old Senate. And the other was that you have certain senators who don't like treaties at all—Rand Paul and some of those folks who, philosophically, are not internationalists by any stretch of the imagination—and the other fact was that we only had one hearing. It was a last-minute deal ... and it just wasn't the right way to handle something of that significance. And the third reason was in committee what we thought was an agreement to wait until next year and debate it when the new Senate was in place. I believe in keeping your commitment. My objection was to the way it was handled.[5]

Isakson based his vote against ratification squarely on the timing of the ratification vote, as did his Republican colleague, Mike Lee of Utah. But Lee, in a statement, provided additional reasons for voting down the treaty, which may have been at least as influential.

The first identified a clause in the treaty that created an independent committee within the UN to make recommendations on measures to help the disabled. "In the past," Lee said, "similar independent committees have made demands of state parties that fall outside the legal, social, economic, and cultural traditions of state parties."[6] Simply put, Senator Lee regarded at least one provision of the treaty as an infringement on US sovereignty.

He followed that with a charge that a provision in the treaty posed a threat to parental rights, and that the treaty set "a precedent for treaties that would actually allow an international body to define its own domestic law." Also, because of the treaty language that "provide[s] persons with disabilities with the same range, quality, and standard of free or affordable health care ... in the area of sexual and reproductive health and population-based public health programs,"[7] Senator Lee charged that "abortion itself falls under 'sexual and reproductive health' and therefore would fall under the requirements of this language."[8]

Conservative religious groups had made known their opposition to the treaty on the same grounds as Senator Lee, although they usually made no mention of the propriety of ratification during a lame-duck session. The *Baptist Press*, for example, noted that an "article in the treaty making 'the best interests of the child' a 'primary consideration' could, in the words of the Home School Legal Defense Association, 'usurp the traditional fundamental right of parents to direct the education and upbringing of a special needs child.'"[9]

John Kerry, according to his own account, stayed up late the night before the floor debate on the treaty, searching Twitter for comments on the treaty, and "spent some time reading the tweets of folks who [didn't] yet agree we should approve the treaty." Point by point Kerry attempted to refute the objections. He first denied that the UN commission that was empowered by the treaty to make recommendations was an infringement on US sovereignty by pointing out that its recommendations were non-binding on the signatory nations. He then challenged the argument that the lame-duck session was not the occasion for a treaty vote by pointing out that since 1970, the Senate had approved nineteen treaties in lame-duck sessions. He did not specifically refute the charges that the rights of home-schoolers would be infringed upon nor that the treaty promoted abortion.[10]

Kerry was well aware of the nature of opposition to the treaty before his evening of sifting through tweets. Five of the six members of the Foreign Relations Committee who had voted against reporting out the bill to the full Senate on July 31, 2012, had gone on record opposing the treaty and set their opinions forth in the portion of the committee report devoted to minority views. These were Republicans James E. Risch of Idaho, Marco Rubio of Florida, James Inhofe of Oklahoma, Jim DeMint of South Carolina, and Mike Lee of Utah. The vote to report out the measure, however, was bipartisan, with ranking member Richard G. Lugar along with Georgia's Johnny Isakson and John Barrasso of Wyoming voting in favor. Curiously, one Republican senator seemed to lie low. Tennessee's Bob Corker did not join his colleagues in their minority views and voted against reporting out the treaty.[11]

Bipartisanship after Defeat

The deep disappointment of treaty supporters was mitigated, to a degree, by two features of the treaty vote. The first is that it was bipartisan and came breathtakingly close to passing. The other was the gender composition of the vote: with one exception, every female senator of both parties supported the treaty. There was also the speech delivered by John McCain on the day after the failed ratification vote at the annual summit of the Human Rights First organization in Washington, DC.

After laying the lash on President Obama for the shortcomings of his human rights policy in such places as Libya and Syria, McCain, barely restraining his anger, berated his Republican colleagues:

I wish I could say that my own party was offering a better alternative to these and other policies. I wish I could say that Republicans were providing moral leadership in the world where the Administration is not. But sadly, in so many instances we are not.... Yesterday was an instructive example. As you know, Senate Republicans voted down the Convention on the Rights of Persons with Disabilities. I understand and respect my colleagues' concerns for American sovereignty and the primacy of our laws. But if ever there were a treaty tailor-made for the advocates of American sovereignty, it was the Disabilities Convention. The treaty would not constrain American sovereignty; it would expand it. It would extend the protection of human rights on which America has proudly led the world for decades. It would demand that the world be more like America. And yet, on the basis of outright falsehoods and fear-mongering, the treaty was voted down.[12]

Democrats, who unanimously supported the treaty, were obviously disappointed by its defeat, but it cannot be claimed that the votes—both in committee and on the Senate floor—were starkly polarized. The Republicans, in fact, would have a better argument that polarization was at work due to the fact that no Democrat broke ranks to oppose the treaty.

The treaty, on its face, might seem unexceptionable, and voting against it would appear to be a slap in the face of the handicapped, but in practical terms it would have accomplished little. Other than making the United States a party to an international convention and presenting the Americans with Disabilities Act as a standard to which the nations of the world were urged to aspire, it contained no appropriation of money for curb-cuts in Cambodia or ramps in Rwanda. It could be characterized as well intentioned but toothless. Republicans might also view it as "message" legislation designed to show their party up as uncaring and callous. Even a Republican who did not buy into the warnings that the treaty promoted abortion or interfered with the homeschooling of special-needs children might have wondered whether it was worth the floor time of the Senate at a time when the nation faced a fiscal crisis in the late fall of 2012.

What does the ratification vote tell us about bipartisanship in the Senate? It certainly does not prove that bipartisanship is extinct. Neither, however, does it make a convincing case that it is terribly robust. Ultimately, though, drawing bright lines to demarcate what is partisan and what is bipartisan can be frustrating.

Votes in the Senate on final passage of bills is undeniably polarized.[13] The party-unity scores—the compilation of votes that show the percentage of roll-call votes on which a majority of Democrats oppose a majority of Republicans—would have us conclude that the Senate is no less partisan that the House.

Yet, before and beneath these roll-call votes on the final passage of legislation, there is considerable bipartisan cooperation at the committee level, innumerable amounts of routine business that is disposed of by unanimous consent, cordial and cooperative relationships between senators of starkly different political philosophies, and even examples of major pieces of legislation that receive substantial, and not token, bipartisan majorities.

In the 112th Congress (2011–2013), when Congress—most conspicuously the House—received an influx of new members supported by the Tea Party, the Senate was able to pass an agriculture bill, a highway bill, and a postal reform bill with substantial bipartisan majorities.

It makes better copy for journalists and even scholars to advance the picture of a dysfunctional Senate. Conflict has long been known to attract more eyes than cooperation.

In the following chapters I will attempt to answer the question "Is Bipartisanship Dead?" not by exaggerating the number or importance of acts of bipartisanship, but rather to describe for the reader just what a complex and subtle phenomenon bipartisanship is. I will not stretch the interpretation of events to see bipartisanship where it may exist only in trifling, exiguous quantities. There are sow's ears from which no silk purse can possibly be made, and a climate of arrant partisanship will not be ignored.

I choose the Senate, not only because it is the institution I have studied for thirty-five years, but because bipartisanship is more central to the existence of that institution than it is in its sister chamber, the House of Representatives—a majoritarian chamber in its very nature, where a determined majority can, under most circumstances, work its will.

2
COMITY CLUBS

SENATE COMMITTEES

Committees are one of the most prominent features of Congress. The forty permanent (standing) committees—twenty in each chamber—present us with a kind of wiring diagram of the policy areas over which Congress exercises jurisdiction. In these areas, which range from agriculture to veterans' affairs, Congress's committees have the power to exercise oversight and to legislate.

Not all committees are created equal. Some exercise great power (the House Rules Committee) while others have modest influence (the Senate Rules Committee). With a few exceptions, the prestige of committees is variable. Both the Senate and House Appropriations Committees, traditionally the most sought-after committees, lost much of their attractiveness to members early in the twenty-first century. There are several reasons for the declining lure of these committees: the abandonment of earmarks, the traditional ability of members to direct federal spending to favored projects; the inability of the committees to get individual spending bills passed except as part of "omnibus" legislation drafted by party leadership; and the recurrent use of continuing resolutions at the end of a fiscal year when the twelve regular appropriations bills have not been passed. The attractiveness of committees is also influenced by the members' own goals. Some are persuaded to seek a committee assignment because of its effect on their reelection chances, others choose committees that enhance their prestige within their chamber, and still others choose a certain committee because they are interested in the areas of legislation for which the committee is responsible.[1]

Forty years ago, Richard F. Fenno, Jr., one of the most respected scholars of the US Congress, studied six committees in the US House of Representatives and found distinctive patterns of partisanship and bipartisanship. He identified four factors that influenced the level of partisanship: the jurisdictions of the committees as set forth in the rules of the House and the related factor of the external constituencies who have an interest in the subjects that fall within that jurisdiction. This was referred to by Fenno as the committee's "policy environment." The third factor he identified was the membership of the committee, most notably the chair and the most senior (ranking) minority member. A fourth, which is both a cause and an effect of partisanship, was the extent to which the goals of the committee members comport with those of party leaders.[2]

This last factor relates to "committee autonomy," the degree to which a committee's members operating within their own policy environment can or cannot bring their committee's actions in line with those of party leaders. Committee members are the reigning specialists on the policies within their committee's jurisdiction, while party leaders are usually generalists whose responsibilities extend broadly to the supervision of the twenty permanent committees. There is often considerable tension between the committee's desire to satisfy the constituencies within its policy environment, and the partisan and ideological goals of the party leaders and the broader national objectives of their party, particularly its more ideological base.

An agriculture committee and its farm-state members who are inclined to be generous with direct payments and price supports for farmers may run afoul of leaders seeking to redeem a national party pledge to reduce the cost of the federal government. This conflict becomes especially acute when there is little ideological diversity in the party. If the dominant ideology in a congressional party favors drastic cuts in federal spending, committees whose members don't conform to that ideology are likely to be fiercely resisted by leaders acting on behalf of the predominant party group. Also, "as the majority party becomes more unified internally about the major issues of the day and the gulf between the policy preferences of the majority and minority party members widens, party leaders become more central to the legislative process and the autonomy of committees tends to decline. Conversely, lower levels of partisan polarization are associated with stronger committees."[3]

Committee colleagues of different parties, especially if they have served together for considerable time, develop close personal ties that transcend party. In addition, as Fenno noted, on some House committees, the region of the country that a member represented trumped partisanship. One Democrat from a western state on the House Interior Committee told Fenno that on his committee, "You're more likely to have geographical partisanship or regional partisanship than party partisanship. I have more in common with a Republican from Montana than with a Democrat from Florida."[4]

Fenno's western Democrat obviously represented a constituency that resembled the congressional district of the Montana Republican much more closely than it did the Floridian from his own party. And since getting reelected figures prominently in the minds of legislators, responsiveness to constituents would be a paramount concern to lawmakers. A conflict between ideology and responsiveness to the constituency would present a dilemma, but one that usually gets resolved in favor of the constituency. Every party leader in Congress is aware of that and is usually respectful of the reelection needs of their party colleagues. But, from time to time, members come under pressure from party leaders, including the head of their own party, to "take one for the team"—a step that most politicians would prefer to avoid.

Much in Congress has changed in the four decades since Fenno wrote. The most conspicuous change has been in the intensity of partisanship in its most intense form—the polarization and the diminishing ideological diversity in both parties. Yet despite the increasing antagonism across party lines, some committees of both the House and Senate, while never wholly free of partisanship, are able to accomplish significant work on a bipartisan basis. But many of Fenno's observations remain valid today, not only for the House but for the US Senate as well.

Reasonably accurate evaluations can be made about committees in the US Senate in their degree of partisanship simply on the basis of their jurisdiction. So if we knew nothing more about a Senate committee than its formal jurisdiction, we could make a pretty fair guess about its level of partisanship. You would be on firm ground if you predicted that the Senate Judiciary Committee would be more partisan than the Senate Agriculture Committee because the former deals with such explosive issues as gun control and abortion and the latter deals with issues of importance to the rural constituents of that committee's members. The Agriculture Committee is more likely to divide by what commodity the constituents produce rather than by what ideology their representatives espouse. To put it another way, a Republican rice farmer may have more in common with a Democratic rice farmer than he does with a Republican wheat farmer.

Partisanship in a committee, however, is not a constant and is highly dependent on factors unrelated to formal jurisdiction. So while the jurisdiction of a Senate committee changes only on rare occasions, the committee's external constituencies and the level of partisan conflict and bipartisan cooperation can change, sometimes quite dramatically, based upon two developments: a change in the committee's leadership and a change in its membership.

The reputation for bipartisanship on the Foreign Relations Committee prior to 2013 had much to do with the ranking Republican, Richard Lugar of Indiana. Lugar was defeated in a Republican primary in 2012. A Democratic staff member, interviewed during the lame-duck session of the outgoing 112th Congress, expressed guarded optimism that Lugar's likely replacement, Bob Corker of Tennessee, might carry on that tradition: "Our committee is moderate because Lugar is such a moderate. I don't think that there is a huge amount of partisanship because of Lugar.... Corker is no extremist, but I think he is being challenged."[5]

This staffer suggested that the challenge faced by Corker was the result of developments well beyond the boundaries of the committee itself, an emerging division within the Republican Party over America's role in the world.

> I think what we're starting to see is multiple splits within the Republican Party on foreign policy. I came into Congress around the start of the Iraq War, and you had Republicans pretty much united on foreign policy, backing Bush. There was a very aggressive internationalist foreign policy by neo-cons [neo-conservatives], but it was a very internationalist foreign policy. It was a policy that I disagreed with, but people were interested in being engaged in the world. What happened was the growth of the Tea Party. I think it's sort of simplistic to say that it's just neo-cons versus Tea Partiers. What's happened is

that an extreme isolationist wing of the party has sprung up and has begun exerting control over the people who are the moderates.[6]

As it turned out, Corker worked cooperatively with the new chairman, Robert Menendez of New Jersey, for eighteen months. The two agreed, for example, that committee members would not introduce legislation without prior bipartisan negotiation.

But in the early spring of 2014, when Russia annexed Crimea from Ukraine, the committee gave bipartisan support to a bill to impose sanctions on Russia. But the committee fell into disagreement over whether Russia's actions in eastern Ukraine warranted stronger sanctions. The Republicans' response was to offer their own sanctions bill without prior negotiations with the Democrats. This drew a strong rebuke from Menendez, who complained, "Their bill is highly political. Everything we've done on this committee up to now has had a bipartisan effort to it. Even introductions of bills have come after negotiations. They're just trying to make political hay on this."[7]

While it is true that some committee jurisdictions are inherently less contentious than others, especially those known as "constituency" committees such as Agriculture, changes in committee personnel and changes in national politics can alter, even if only temporarily, the partisan tone of a committee.

One Senate committee long-considered among the most bipartisan is the Senate Armed Services Committee, which experienced substantial change in both leadership and membership in 2013 with the start of the 113th Congress.

Peace and War on the Senate Armed Services Committee

There is a consensus among journalists who cover Congress that the Senate Armed Services Committee has had a long tradition of bipartisanship.[8] Chaired since 2007 by Senator Carl Levin (D-MI), its ranking Republican member in the 112th Congress was Senator John McCain (R-AZ). A member of the committee during that Congress, Senator Mark Begich (D-AK) agreed that ideology was not a controlling factor on the committee:

> It's more about military defense. That is the common denominator. We have pretty fierce policy debates on things like missile defense in Europe, but at the end of the day, for as long as I've been there, we get to a solution. We have two strong-willed chairs (Levin and McCain) but they still get through it. We have a couple of days of painful discussion and we're very blunt and honest about it, but at the end of the day we get there and I think that's good.[9]

Viewed from the staff level, the picture was similar:

> Levin and McCain went out of their way to accommodate each other when the two of them had priorities that they really wanted to push on the committee. Often, there were not particularly bipartisan viewpoints or bipartisan issues on the committee, but the two of them always had this approach where they feel they can negotiate a solution that would work for everybody involved.[10]

But this staff member added that although Levin and McCain succeeded in getting agreements on tough issues such as those related to detainees captured in the antiterrorism campaign, the very bipartisan cooperation that they achieved, while a credit to them as committee leaders, "created headaches for their leadership."[11]

From the point of view of party leadership in the Senate, there can be such a thing as too much bipartisanship.

Democratic chairman Levin might have found himself perfectly in accord with ranking Republican McCain, but that bipartisan harmony may not have set well with Majority Leader Harry Reid, who might have wanted a bill more pleasing to the Democratic party base.

When the new Congress convened in January 2013, Republican Party rules that limit the number of terms a ranking member may serve in that capacity required McCain to relinquish his post as ranking member. He was replaced in that position by Senator James Inhofe (R-OK), but McCain remained a committee member.

The membership was also significantly altered. Two moderate New England Republicans, Susan Collins of Maine and Scott Brown of Massachusetts, left the committee, as did Rob Portman of Ohio and John Cornyn of Texas. They were replaced by Republicans who were markedly more conservative.

The new members were Deb Fischer of Nebraska, Mike Lee of Utah, Ted Cruz of Texas, and Roy Blunt of Missouri. Leaving the committee were Democrats Jim Webb of Virginia and Ben Nelson of Nebraska, along with independent Joseph Lieberman, who caucused with the democrats. They were replaced by Democrats Joe Donnelly of Indiana, Tim Kaine of Virginia, and Mazie Hirono of Hawaii, plus independent Angus King of Maine. As a House member, Senator Hirono was characterized as having "a solidly liberal voting record" and a one-time Republican opponent described her as "too liberal even for Hawaii."[12] The Republican newcomers, on the whole, made the Republican side of the panel substantially more conservative. On the Democratic side, the freshmen turned the dial ever so slightly in the liberal direction. These changes, along with an intensifying antipathy of Republicans to President Obama's nominations, engendered opposition on this committee to the nomination of a former fellow senator, Republican Chuck Hagel.[13]

Savaging Sergeant Hagel

At a White House briefing on January 7, 2013, President Barack Obama announced, simultaneously, the retirement of Leon Panetta as secretary of defense and the nomination of Panetta's successor, Nebraska's ex-senator Chuck Hagel.[14] The hearings on nominations of Pentagon officials fall under the jurisdiction of the Senate Armed Services Committee.

In many ways Hagel seemed a natural choice for the job. His two terms as a Republican senator would send a strong bipartisan message to the Senate Armed Services Committee members who would be holding his confirmation hearings. In addition to his prior Senate service, Hagel had served as a combat infantryman in Vietnam, where he had been twice wounded and had received a pair of Purple Heart decorations. In the Senate, he had served on both the Foreign Relations and Intelligence Committees, although never on Armed Services. There were, however, complicating factors in the nomination involving the former ranking Republican on the committee, Senator John McCain.

McCain had campaigned vigorously for Hagel in Nebraska in 1996, and in 2000 Hagel returned the favor by endorsing McCain for the Republican presidential nomination. It was a step on Hagel's part that put him at odds with most Senate Republicans who, with only four exceptions, were backing Governor George W. Bush of Texas. Hagel paid a political price for backing McCain, his friend and fellow Vietnam War veteran. By 2001 he was feeling isolated within the Republican caucus. Bush had won the presidency, and Hagel felt the need to repair his relations with the White House and get back in good standing with his fellow Republicans.[15]

It was at this time that McCain introduced a bipartisan campaign-finance reform bill with Senator Russ Feingold, a Wisconsin Democrat. Republican Leader Trent Lott and

Senator Mitch McConnell (later to be Republican leader) were implacable foes of the McCain-Feingold bill and close allies of the Bush White House. Hagel, rather than backing McCain-Feingold, drew up his own campaign-finance bill that covered many of the same areas as McCain-Feingold but omitted a major feature of it. The Hagel bill did find favor with Lott, McConnell, and the White House, who saw it as a way to undercut McCain. Hagel evidently saw it as a way to ingratiate himself with the Republican leaders. McCain saw this as an act of betrayal.[16]

So the Hagel-McCain relationship was problematic on a personal level, but Hagel and McCain had also stood on opposite sides of a major foreign policy issue, the decision by President George W. Bush to augment the US force in Iraq with a "surge" of 30,000 troops in the spring of 2007. McCain saw the surge as a war-winning strategy. Hagel denounced the surge on the floor of the Senate as "the most dangerous blunder in this country since Vietnam."[17] Hagel faced other obstacles to his nomination, as well, including a belief that he was insufficiently supportive of Israel and too conciliatory toward Iran.

By most accounts, Hagel performed poorly in his testimony before the Armed Services Committee on January 31, 2012. His answers often seemed tentative, and Hagel appeared evasive under the hectoring of McCain about whether or not the Iraq surge had been effective. But the only voices calling for him to withdraw were Republican. With fifty-five Democrats backing him, Hagel was certain to be confirmed unless, of course, the Republicans filibustered the nomination. Two weeks later, on February 12, 2013, Senator Levin convened a business meeting of the twenty-six-member Armed Services Committee in room 222 of the Russell Senate Office Building.

As is customary in Senate hearings, the chairman made the opening statement, and Levin praised the president's nomination of Hagel. As is also customary, the next statement was made by the ranking minority member, in this case Senator James Inhofe, who made a perfunctory reference to Hagel's heroism but quickly announced that he would oppose the nomination. The statements then followed in the order of the seniority of the members on the committee, alternating between Democrats and Republicans. When the turn came to Senator Lindsey Graham, a South Carolina Republican, he added a little bipartisan emollient by saying, "This is a good committee, and we got a good chairman. We have a good ranking member. I like my colleagues." Then, he contrasted the overwhelming bipartisan vote given to Democratic senator John Kerry for secretary of state with the treatment that Hagel, a Republican, was getting at the hands of Republicans: "It's the times in which we live. The Democrats are not going to get almost universal support from Republicans and the Republicans are going to get almost no Republican support."[18]

Until this point, nothing had been heard from the committee's most junior member, Senator Ted Cruz (R-TX). His initial statement acknowledged the committee's bipartisan history and he expressed satisfaction at becoming a member, but he then moved in a very different direction by accusing Hagel of "giving speeches at extreme or radical groups" and intimated that he had "accepted financial compensation" from them. Cruz quickly added that he had no evidence that Hagel had ever made such speeches or accepted money, but he hinted that Hagel's refusal to disclose the source of all of his speaking fees suggested that Hagel had something to hide.[19]

This elicited a sharp rejoinder from Chairman Levin, who pointed out to Senator Cruz that Hagel had submitted all of the disclosure forms required of him according to committee rules and that if Cruz wanted to propose a change to those rules he could, "but it's not going to be a separate rule for Senator Hagel than it is for all the other nominees." Levin added,

"We are not going to single out one nominee for this kind of disparate treatment."[20]

At this point, alarms bells were going off that the vaunted bipartisanship of the committee was being jolted by a new-comer, and Senator Bill Nelson (D-FL) jumped in to chide Cruz:

> There is a certain degree of comity and civility that this committee has always been known for. And clearly, in the sharpness of difference of opinion to question, in essence, whether someone is a fellow traveler [the implication that Hagel was acting as a kind of stooge] for another country, I think, is taking it too far. And I would encourage the committee to take the role model of its former chairman, Senator McCain, who can get into it hot and heavy, but at the end of the day, he is going to respect the other person's motives. And I would implore the committee to consider that.[21]

But Cruz was not without his defenders, as James Inhofe entered the discussion by saying, "I think I wrote down the words [by Bill Nelson] criticizing our senator [Cruz] for implying that Chuck Hagel was cozy with terrorist-type countries," referring to Iran. "Let me say, I would say, he is endorsed by them. You can't get any cozier than that." To that, Levin replied archly, "I have been endorsed by people I disagree with totally. I don't want people who hate me to ruin my career by endorsing me."[22]

Hagel then received bipartisan support from an unexpected quarter. John McCain, the Arizona Republican and Hagel's estranged friend who had badgered Hagel on the witness stand, lashed out at Cruz: "I just want to make it clear. Senator Hagel is an honorable man. He has served his country. And no one on this committee at any time should impugn his character or his integrity."[23]

Boutique Bipartisanship: Comity in Committees

It has been noted that bipartisanship varies from committee to committee. Certain distinctive features of virtually all Senate committees affect bipartisan cooperation. The first is the relationship between seniority and bipartisanship.

By the time senators achieve seniority on a committee, it may be assumed that they are exactly where they want to be. Newly elected senators may request seats on committees of their choice, but the party steering committees that are responsible for assignments may place them where there are vacancies rather than where the newcomers prefer to be. Over time, however, senators who have served more than a single six-year term tend to get committee assignments that are to their liking. By the time that a senator has risen to chairmanship or ranking member status, he or she has a great deal invested in the committee. Senior senators can be expected to defend the jurisdictions of their committee against incursions from other chairmen who seek to peel off parts of its jurisdiction. They work to enhance the committee's prestige and influence. They are also concerned with "quality of life" on the committee. Clashing repeatedly with colleagues in disputes unmodulated by civility is unappealing to those who head committees.

Critical to the functioning of a committee is the relationship between the senator who chairs the committee and the ranking minority member. Senate committee chairs possess great power and can wield it unilaterally. They can decide whether a bill that is referred to committee will have hearings and thus launch it on its way or call no hearings and have the bill die. They also control the manner in which hearings are held in such a way as either to help the bill or to derail it. This authority enables them to choose the day of the hearings and to determine the witness list and the order in which witnesses testify. They also heavily influence the amendment process in the committee (markup) by accepting some amendments and rejecting others.

An example of the broad powers wielded by a committee chair was the response of the Armed Services Committee to a Pentagon report on the sexual assault problem in the military. This issue found Democratic chairman Carl Levin at odds with one of the most liberal Democrats on the committee, Senator Kirsten Gillibrand of New York, over whether the prosecution of service members accused of sexual assault should be taken out of the hands of commanders and placed in the hands of military lawyers. Levin stoutly defended the military chain of command and "at a hearing [he] . . . compiled a witness list of people who supported keeping the prosecution of sexual assault cases within the chain of command as Ms. Gillibrand pushed to hear from more victims' advocates. She and others took the witness list as a sign that Mr. Levin was stacking the deck."[24]

Committee chairs can also decide what kind of relationship they want to have with their ranking minority members. Relations between these senior senators can be close and consultative or distant or even fractious. All of the senators I interviewed who were either committee chairs or ranking members reported good relationships with their counterparts of the other party and stressed the importance of such relationships.

Chairs and ranking members share a feeling of proprietorship. The relationship between the two senators, who reach this status by reason of the length of their service on the committee, is critical to the success of the committee. By the time a senator becomes the chair or the ranking member, he or she has a great deal invested in the committee and usually goes to great pains to forge good collegial relationships with his or her counterparts.

Senator Debbie Stabenow (D-MI) and Senator Pat Roberts (R-KS) were chair and ranking member, respectively, of the Agriculture Committee in the 112th Congress. Stabenow described her approach to working with Roberts:

I worked very hard to get to know Senator Roberts. We spent time together. I went to Kansas and he came to Michigan. We really learned about each other's states and agriculture needs and we had people on both sides of the committee who cared deeply about agriculture and had a lot of experience.[25]

When Roberts was compelled to step down from his position as ranking member because of the Republican Party rules on term limits for how long a Republican senator can serve as either chair or ranking member, Stabenow immediately made overtures to her new ranking member, Senator Thad Cochran (R-MS):

For me, the ability to go to my ranking member's state is crucial in the relationship. It's now Senator Cochran, and I am going to Mississippi. He has invited me down to speak to a very prestigious agricultural group down there—the Delta Council—and I have been happy to accept and have a chance to visit with growers, and I really welcome the opportunity. I think that's important for me to do, and I am inviting him to Michigan as well. It's important to understand the perspective of the people you're working with.[26]

It is important to note that Agriculture has long enjoyed the reputation of being one of the Senate committees least affected by excessive partisanship. As Stabenow explained, "It's definitely a more bipartisan committee by its nature. There tend to be regional disagreements, so Southerners have a different view of farm policy from those in the Northwest or Midwest. It's more regional than ideological."[27] This view was seconded by staff members, who reported that the bipartisanship extends to committee staff as well: "I'm really good friends with my Republican counterpart. I go out and have drinks with him. I love that dude. He and I could cut a deal tomorrow that would be a good deal and get a farm bill."[28]

A farm bill was what was reported out of the Agriculture Committee in the 112th Congress. Stabenow and Roberts fashioned a bill that was acceptable to the senators advocating for their own growers and ranchers. It did not, however, get very far in the House, where resistance within the Republican caucus to the price tag on the bill was too steep for conservatives to accept, even though there was considerable support within the House Agriculture Committee itself.

The right personal chemistry can smooth over the rough edges even on the committee with the reputation of being the Senate's most contentious. Patrick Leahy (D-VT), chairman of the Judiciary Committee, explained his approach:

> I use my hideaway office with the balcony overlooking the Mall. I do that a lot for meetings with both Democrats and Republicans. If it's an evening session, I have a bar open and we'll have a cocktail hour there. As one senator said to another, "We're going down for prayer hour and holy water in Pat's office." The second senator said, "But I'm Jewish." And the first one said, "You get your choice between twelve-year-old or single-malt holy water." And the second senator said, "I'll convert."[29]

These contemporary reports about the relative harmony on the Agriculture Committee sound remarkably similar to the testimony that Richard Fenno received from House Interior Committee members more than four decades ago.[30]

Even more impressively, a Senate committee headed by an unlikely pair of senators also managed to produce a major piece of legislation authorizing infrastructure projects. This was the Committee on Environment and Public Works, whose chairwoman was Senator Barbara Boxer (D-CA), by nearly any measure one of the most liberal members of the Senate.

Her counterpart and ranking member, Senator James Inhofe
(R-OK), was ranked in 2010 by the National Journal as the
most conservative member of the Senate.[31]

Senator Boxer described the process of building a working
relationship with Senator Inhofe:

> I think the first thing to decide as soon as I got the gavel
> was which areas Inhofe and I actually agree on and be
> very, very honest about it, to sit down with him, as we did
> on many occasions. And we knew, for example, that on
> environmental protection we couldn't be further apart.
> And that was a known fact. And so rather than declare
> open war on it, we decided to respect each other's dif-
> ferences and we never hesitated to criticize each other's
> views, but we didn't take it personally. And, believe me,
> we had some very difficult moments because I think that
> climate change is one of the greatest threats we face. He
> thinks it is one of the biggest hoaxes we've ever seen. So
> there's no room there.
>
> Then we realized that we shared a great interest in
> rebuilding the nation's transportation system. He believes
> that that's a function of government—one of the few—and
> I agree because I believe it is one of the important func-
> tions but also because I see it as a way to make sure the
> economy keeps humming.... So, knowing that we had
> that in common, we sat down to write our transportation
> bill.[32]

At the end of our interview, Senator Boxer looked ahead to
the 113th Congress and expressed the hope that she and her
new ranking member, David Vitter of Louisiana, would be able
to work as harmoniously together as she and Senator Inhofe did.

The beginning of the new Congress seemed to confirm
Senator Boxer's hope. Vitter announced that he would "very
much [be] following the relationship and lead of Barbara Boxer

and Jim Inhofe, my predecessor."[33] She and Vitter introduced a water infrastructure bill in March 2013. When the bill passed the Senate in May, Boxer said that "when it comes to the infrastructure of our country, we come together."[34]

Shortly thereafter, Vitter organized opposition to President Obama's nomination of a new director of the Environmental Protection Agency. This would not be an unusual stand for a senator from an oil-producing state to take, but he followed that with an amendment to an energy bill that would strip the subsidy for health insurance provided under the Affordable Care Act ("Obamacare") from members of Congress and their staffs. Democrats retaliated by offering an amendment of their own that would deny subsidies to senators for whom there was evidence of probable cause that they had solicited prostitutes, a reference to a 2007 revelation that Vitter's name had been found in the address book of a woman known as "the DC Madam."[35]

The Boxer-Vitter clash tells us that harmonious committee relationships can be fragile. Even committees with long-standing reputations as havens of bipartisanship can erupt into discord. A Republican senator who requested anonymity served on the Intelligence Committee, which has in recent years enjoyed a reputation (perhaps exaggerated) for bipartisanship. This senator spoke of the harmony on other committees on which he served but could not say the same of Intelligence:

> Intelligence was a disaster. Pat Roberts and [Jay] Rockefeller were about as far apart ideologically and personally, backgrounds, socially, culturally as they could be. And they didn't even try to zip it up. It was really rough. It was very uncomfortable. Then [Kit] Bond (R-MO) took over. Bond was even worse than Roberts. It was the *Wild Kingdom.*[36]

So while it is not universally true that committees are havens of bipartisanship in a polarized world, the relative intimacy of the committee—the attraction of a committee's jurisdiction to senators, the closeness that develops among members over time, especially among the ranking members—promotes a familiarity that can breed not contempt but, surprisingly often, bipartisanship.

Accepting the reality of this "boutique bipartisanship" begs a few questions. The first of these is, how important are these bills that are the product of committee bipartisanship? Is our standard for accomplishment in the contemporary Senate so dismally low that we celebrate the passage through committee of routine reauthorization bills as if they were landmark legislation? The second is, if the bipartisan legislation cannot survive beyond the committee and fails to get floor action for final passage, how much is really accomplished?

As the bill is reported out from the committee where bipartisan action is common, it enters an environment with a dramatically different dynamic. The Senate floor is much more highly charged and typically a more partisan environment, where offering amendments to a bill may have less to do with improving legislation than with delivering a message designed to damage the opposing party.

The survival of bipartisanship in Senate committees is acknowledged by congressional scholar Sean Theriault in an otherwise pessimistic appraisal of Senate bipartisanship. He acknowledges that "one place where the partisan war is not yet raging is in committees. While Senate committees certainly see more contentious fights than they did before, they still on occasion offer the floor bipartisan solutions to public policy problems. On the floor, though, they get trapped in the partisan war and, like Senate moderates, end up as collateral damage."[37] He then adds this ominous note: "The next battlefront in the war may very well be the committees."[38]

3
BIG-BOX BIPARTISANSHIP AND BOUTIQUE BIPARTISANSHIP

As we have seen within the Senate committee system, bipartisanship in the US Senate is conditional. Under certain circumstances and in certain venues, it has some vitality, while in others it is less frequent and more unpredictable.

But as we saw in the previous chapter, in the intimate confines of a Senate committee, personal ties and common interests promote bipartisanship. But these committees are Congress's "policy boutiques"—specialty shops that attract a distinctive clientele of "outliers," whose views may not be typical of all senators, even those in their own party.

As we have seen, committees such as Agriculture are regionally biased toward states where crops and livestock occupy a prominent place. Armed Services, although it includes within its jurisdiction the broad issue of national defense, is a committee that would naturally attract senators who represent states with a large economic stake in the defense budget through the

bases or aerospace and/or other industries located there. The
state of Maine always has a senator on Armed Services to stand
guard over the interests of the Bath Iron Works, a builder of
warships for the US Navy.

On occasion, legislation can survive even to the point of
passage in the chamber coming out of the committee with a
strong bipartisan vote. Some examples are the infrastructure
and agriculture bills and the postal reform bill reported out by
the Government Affairs Committee in the 112th Congress.
But these bills, however important, don't touch the overarching issues of American politics. None of them addressed the
budgetary issues that define the scope and cost of the federal
government. Tax and spending matters are the "big box" issues
that define the ideological battle lines of American politics and
are the issues most likely to generate hyperpartisanship and
polarization. The Committee on the Budget is foremost among
the Senate committees in which ideological combat is the norm.

Alaska Democrat Mark Begich serves on four committees:
Armed Services, Budget, Commerce, and Homeland Security.
I asked him to single out the committee that was the most
partisan. He replied, "It's Budget that's obviously contentious
because there are philosophical differences on what our priorities ought to be." Michigan Democrat Debbie Stabenow contrasted her service on Budget with her membership on Finance:
"Budget is a different place, because in the Budget Committee
today, in the large ideological and philosophical sense, there are
very different views as to what is most important for the government to do. . . . In my thirteen years on Budget, the budget has
always come down to a partisan vote. In the Finance Committee
we see a lot more attempts to work across the aisle."[1]

There is a historical irony in the fact that contemporary
senators regard the Budget Committee as the least bipartisan.
Established by the Budget Act of 1975, the committee was
initially the very model of bipartisanship under its first leaders,

Edmund Muskie (D-ME) and Henry Bellmon (R-OK). The tradition was carried for a time by their immediate successors, but it has become increasingly partisan.

So although there are significant exceptions to the general principle that there is considerable bipartisanship on the committees of the Senate, it would be safe to say that the world of committees is a less contentious place than the Senate floor. The committee is the realm of "regular order," the systematic and methodical processing of legislation by policy specialists backed up by professional committee staffs. The Senate floor is a more freewheeling place of political combat, of partisan cut and thrust, and a place where, in a time of political polarization, points can be scored against the opposition.

Floor Action and Inaction

The Senate's consideration of the UN Convention on the Rights of the Disabled, which was discussed at the beginning of this book, illustrates the fact that the atmosphere of partisanship can change quite dramatically when a bill leaves a committee and reaches the floor of the Senate. The treaty, you will recall, was reported out of the Foreign Relations Committee on a 13–6 bipartisan vote and failed to attain the required two-thirds majority for ratification, losing the votes of some of the senators who had voted in committee to improve it.

When legislation moves from the confines of the committee to the floor, according to Virginia Democrat Mark Warner, "it's open season."[2]

For Senator John Boozman, an Arkansas Republican, "There is just a different dynamic on the floor. On the floor—unlike the committee, where you roll up your sleeves and get work done—it's more posturing to a national audience, and that creates problems with both sides posturing to their base."[3]

Put most directly, by Nebraska Republican Mike Johanns, "What is happening is that we are forgetting how to work together on the floor."[4]

Why is the floor dynamic so different from that in committee?

To begin with, debate is unlimited. Under Senate Rule XXII, the delay of a bill can continue indefinitely unless sixty senators vote to end debate with a cloture vote. Such obstruction, in its extreme form, the filibuster, may also be used simply to extract concessions for the benefit of an individual senator. In contrast, committee hearings set time limits on senators' questions to witnesses, and committee voting is by simple majority.

Second, the amending process is unstructured. Amendments can be offered by any senator at any time, and the amendments need not be pertinent (or germane) to the bill being amended. This leads to the use of "message amendments" that can be used to promote a partisan theme or to force members of the opposition to go on record in favor of the amendment or opposed to it. To increase the chances of such amendments passing the Senate, they are often attached to "vehicles," legislation so critical that it will be adopted even with the mischievous amendments.

In February 2012, the US Department of Health and Human Services issued a directive requiring religious-affiliated hospitals and other institutions to offer contraception as part of their health coverage for their employees. The Republican response was to introduce an amendment to the bipartisan transportation bill, a popular measure. The bill's very popularity marked it as a "vehicle" to which a senator would be eager to attach an amendment in the hope that it might pass the Senate along with the amendments that had been added to it. In most instances, however, this type of message legislation rarely passes. Such was the case with the most sweeping amendment, which was offered by Senator Roy Blunt of Missouri and would have forbidden HHS from requiring contraception coverage. The hope on the part of Republicans was to display Democrats as hostile to religion. Ultimately, the Blunt amendment was defeated because of the effectiveness of the Democrats' coun- ternarrative that the amendment was antiwoman.

The power enjoyed by senators to offer amendments designed to put opponents in an uncomfortable spot is especially trouble- some for those senators facing reelection. After the 2010 elec- tion, in which the Democratic majority was reduced from a margin of 55–41 to 51–47 (not including two independents who typically vote with the Democrats), Majority Leader Harry Reid faced a challenge. He needed to protect Democratic sena- tors facing reelection in 2012 and his own position as major- ity leader. Via a parliamentary device known as "filling the amendment tree," Reid used his powers to block amendments designed by the Republicans to embarrass Democrats up for reelection. This is based on the rule that gives the majority leader the right to be recognized first by the presiding office and thus preempt all available amendments. The Republicans retaliated by filibustering legislation backed by Reid and the Obama administration. Reid's strategy was to protect Demo- crats from taking tough votes while going after Republicans for indiscriminate filibustering.

All of the six Republican senators I interviewed complained, in one way or another, about Reid's practice of filling the amendment tree and defended their use of the filibuster as a tool of retaliation. Idaho Republican Mike Crapo said, "One reason we do that [filibuster] is that the majority cuts us out of the process by the majority leader filling the tree, which is happening on the floor just as we are speaking. When he fills the tree it means that Republicans cannot offer amendments … and then the Republicans say, "OK, if you're not going to let us at least debate our amendments, we're not going to let you have the bill."[5]

"In his capacity as majority leader, Reid rarely, if ever, let[s] a major policy battle pass without exercising his scheduling authority to highlight the differences between the parties. The votes forced by Reid … are not so much intended to aid the passage of bills as to allow Democrats to chide Republicans for being obstructionists."[6]

In the spring of 2014, the Democrats were eager to highlight the differences between themselves and the Republicans on the issue of income inequality by pressing for an increase in the federal minimum wage from $7.25 to $10.10 per hour. On the floor of the Senate, Republican Whip John Cornyn gave his own interpretation of what was behind the Democratic push for the increase:

> We all know what is happening here, so let's talk about the eight-hundred-pound gorilla in the Senate chamber. The truth is that the president and Majority Leader Reid don't expect this bill to pass because they are actually very intelligent people and they know the facts as I have just described them. This is all about politics. This is trying to make this side of the aisle look bad and hardhearted to try to rescue this midterm election coming up in November. We know from reporting in *The New York Times* and elsewhere that this minimum wage bill—this show vote we are going to have here shortly—is part of a larger messaging package created in collaboration with the Democratic Senatorial Campaign Committee. That is not me talking; that is the admission by the leadership on the other side of the aisle. This is not about actually solving a problem; this is about political theater, courtesy of Majority Leader Reid.[7]

There is one instance in which messaging amendments continue to proliferate—the budget resolution, which, unlike ordinary legislation, is strictly an internal document for Congress and does not go to the White House for a presidential signature. Nonetheless, the resolution gives rise to so much amending activity that it is known in the Senate as "vote-a-rama." As Virginia Democrat Mark Warner recalls, "I remember the first time I went through one of those budget marathons and agonized a great deal because so many of those amendments were 'gotcha' amendments on both sides. You know, 'When did you stop beating your wife or whoever?' amendments."[8]

Message Politics and Bipartisanship

Political scientist Frances Lee has offered evidence that the near-equivalence in the number of Democrats and Republicans in the Senate in recent years induces senators to offer message amendments that magnify the differences between the parties because the change in just a handful of seats can cause control of the Senate to shift in any two-year period. This promotes what has been called the "permanent campaign" that may have the effect of magnifying polarization. She suggests that "in many cases, the high levels of congressional party conflict may well not represent genuine ideological polarization, a widening disagreement between the parties on basic questions of public policy. Instead, it may simply reflect the ways in which the permanent campaign has transformed congressional floor politics."[9]

Budget and fiscal matters now stand at the fault line of American politics. The national debate over the proper size and role of the federal government is made concrete in budget resolutions, appropriations, and tax bills. Traditionally appropriations and tax bills have been the most heavily lobbied. In the past, interest group activity was focused very tightly on specific provisions of the tax code that might benefit a client, on an appropriations bill that might contain "earmarks" that direct federal spending to a particular state or congressional district at a member's request, or on attaching an amendment to a budget resolution because it is a "vehicle" on which such amendments might hitch a ride to final passage. Most of these amendments were of interest to only a handful of people, rarely attracted media attention, and were often supported by bipartisan coalitions.

Somewhat less common were high-profile bills that touched on the differences between Democrats and Republicans, liberals and conservatives, labor and business. These bills attracted the attention of a few organizations that tallied the votes of members of Congress on ideologically freighted "key votes" and assigned numerical scores to them. A member might boast of having a rating of 100% by the Club for Growth as evidence of his or her opposition to tax increases. Others might point to a similarly strong rating on the key votes of the League of Conservation Voters to vouch for their commitment to the environment.

Not all votes cast by a senator or House member are "scored" by interest groups, but the decision to score a vote on an issue dear to the heart of an interest group can profoundly affect the calculations of a Senate or House member as to whether it should be supported or opposed.

To Score or Not to Score

Scoring normally takes place on recorded votes on the floor of the chamber on which senators and House members go on record as having cast an "aye," a "nay," or a "present." While recorded votes occur in committee, interest groups typically score only floor votes. While much business in the Senate is conducted under unanimous consent agreement, in which all 100 senators support an action (typically a minor procedural matter that would only rarely be scored), recorded votes are tallied meticulously by the representatives of interest groups and used to compile percentages of votes for measures they favor or oppose.

In its biennial issues, the *Almanac of American Politics* provides data on ten interest groups, most of whom score senators and House members on their votes during a two-year Congress. Some of these groups, such as the American Conservative Union and Americans for Democratic Action score members' votes across a broad spectrum of votes that would position a member or a senator on an ideological spectrum from liberal to conservative. Others, such as the League of Conservation Voters and the Information Technology Industry Council score members on a more tightly focused array of issues. The National Rifle Association (NRA) naturally sets its sights on gun rights/gun control votes.

> Before most votes having anything to do with gun rights, and even some that don't, the NRA will announce that they will be "scoring" the vote, meaning that they will take this vote into account when assembling a letter grade to assign to each candidate.... [T]he NRA grades have become a vital part of how candidates portray themselves to voters, and conservative and swing-district members will do anything they can to keep a good rating.[10]

The NRA's disposition to score a vote beyond its usual focus on gun-related bills is seen in its decision in 2009 to score votes on a nomination to the US Supreme Court, something the organization had never before done. The nominee was Judge Sonia Sotomayor, who was nominated by President Obama.

According to one account, Senate Minority Leader Mitch McConnell (R-KY) "asked a favor of his friends at the National Rifle Association: oppose the Sotomayor nomination and, furthermore, 'score' the confirmation vote. Once it announced its opposition and its intention to score the vote, Republican support for the nominee melted away. Only seven Republicans voted for confirmation."[11] Curiously, Sotomayor, as a lower court judge, had never ruled on a case relating to guns. The closest she came was an opinion on the use of nunchaku (i.e., nunchucks).

After the school shooting in Newtown, Connecticut, in December 2012, momentum quickly developed for expanded background checks for gun purchases. In the course of discussions among senators to find a way to enhance background checks that would garner enough votes for passage, a bipartisan bill was produced by Democrat Joe Manchin of West Virginia and Republican Pat Toomey of Pennsylvania. Both senators were seen as NRA allies in the past, but Manchin's reaction to the shooting at the school was influenced by his being a father and grandfather. Toomey was described by one conservative publication as "the best ally they're [the NRA] going to get elected statewide in Pennsylvania."[12]

The Manchin-Toomey amendment on expanded background checks for firearms purchases received only 54 votes. An agreement between the Democratic and Republican leaders set a threshold of 60 votes to pass the amendment. Soon after the vote, Manchin reflected on the defeat and pointed to the moment when it appeared to be doomed: when the National Rifle Association announced that it would score the vote. "If [the NRA] hadn't scored it, we'd have gotten 70 votes," Manchin observed ruefully.[13]

Later in 2013, the NRA again proved decisive on a surprising vote to confirm a permanent director of the Bureau of Alcohol, Tobacco, Firearms, and Explosives (ATF). Since 2006, the NRA had blocked the appointment of a permanent director, and B. Todd Jones was serving as acting director when President Obama nominated him for the permanent job. In a surprising move, the NRA declined to score the vote on Jones.[14] He was subsequently confirmed.

Getting to 60: The Filibuster and Cloture

As Barbara Sinclair has noted, "With the growth in partisan polarization, Republicans and Democrats now frequently use the Senate's permissive rules for partisan purposes."[15] Partisan conflict and its operational counterpart, "the permanent campaign," often find expression not only in message amendments but also in the politics of the filibuster. A parliamentary tactic typically used by the minority party, the filibuster is more likely to find senators of the majority and minority deeply divided than is any piece of substantive legislation. Accordingly, "pressure is placed on senators to vote with their party colleagues."[16]

Filibustering is easy. None of the lengthy speeches or thundering oratory of past decades is required for debate. The process is explained by Majority Leader Harry Reid's deputy chief of staff, Bill Dauster:

> Now senators simply register with their party leader, usually by letter, their objections to the Senate's proceeding to a matter. This objection—called "a hold"—implies the threat of a filibuster should the Senate take up the disputed matter. With the leadership honoring her hold, a senator can be assured that action on the disputed matter will be slowed—even in the senator's absence.[17]

Without the imminent threat of a hold or a filibuster, senators may simply agree to have a 60-vote threshold to take up legislation when there is disagreement over a bill. In May 2014, Majority Leader Reid sought unanimous consent for a 60-vote threshold for a bill supported by Republicans that would have approved the Keystone XL pipeline carrying oil from Alberta, Canada, to the Gulf Coast. This was part of an agreement for another 60-vote threshold on an energy efficiency bill that the Democrats backed.[18]

The Senate is a small institution whose 100 members have responsibility for the same areas of legislation as the 435-member House. This means that senators have broader committee responsibilities than House members, who concentrate their efforts on a single committee. The typical senator serves on three or even four committees and thus can encounter a larger proportion of his or her colleagues in a committee setting. Senate committees are also smaller than House committees, so the intimacy factor is amplified. These opportunities to encounter colleagues in multiple settings give senators a broader acquaintanceship within the chamber.

The value of the Senate's compactness was summed up by Senator Mike Johanns (R-NE):

> I don't know if this is an apt description, but if you can think of a small community or a small high school or whatever, the Senate is a total of only 100 and your caucus may be 45 people. You get to know people pretty well at that level when you're working together every day. These personal relationships are enormously important. It's not like you have a vague perception of what a person may be like. You have actually been in meetings with him. You've seen how he works and your staff has worked with his staff, for good or bad.[19]

The Gangs of the Senate

Since the first years of the twenty-first century, ad hoc bipartisan groups of senators, sometimes consisting of members of a single committee and sometimes unconnected to a committee, have combined to try to circumvent the gridlock produced by partisan polarization. The first of these to gain wide public notice was the Gang of Fourteen, organized in 2005 to prevent a crisis produced by the Democratic minority filibustering President George W. Bush's nominations to the US Court of Appeals.

The Republicans threatened to resort to what they called "the constitutional option" and what the Democrats called "the nuclear option" to win confirmation for the nominees. The option involved the use of a parliamentary device that would have enabled Senate rules to be changed by a simple majority vote rather than the two-thirds typically required by Senate rules. What made the option "nuclear" was the threat by the Democratic minority to obstruct all Senate business. The Gang of Fourteen produced a compromise that blocked the use of the option by allowing some of the nominees to be confirmed.

The confirmation of federal appeals court judges has become one of the most contentious issues facing the Senate. These appellate judges serve for life, so their tenure extends well beyond the term of the president who nominated them, which places the imprint of the president—be that person liberal or conservative—on the decisions of the court for years to come.

While the Gang of Fourteen was successful, "it has been far harder for gangs that want to produce, not just block."[20] In 2007, for example, a Gang of Twelve attempted to break an impasse on immigration reform by assembling a package of compromises. It succeeded in getting only 45 votes.

In 2009, a Gang of Six moderate senators on the Finance Committee spent four months searching for a compromise on health insurance reform, but its efforts failed when Minority Leader Mitch McConnell and Republican Whip John Kyl persuaded two Republican senators, Mike Enzi of Wyoming and Charles Grassley of Iowa, to withdraw from efforts to get Senate approval for the Affordable Care Act (Obamacare).

In 2011, as Congress was facing a vote on an extension of the debt limit, a bipartisan group of six senators (confusingly also dubbed the Gang of Six) was organized to cut $4.6 billion from the deficit. And in 2012, a Gang of Eight was successful in getting the Senate Judiciary committee to support a compromise bill on comprehensive immigration reform.[21]

The emergence of these "gangs" at critical times raises questions: Why have they become so commonplace, and how do they form?

The gangs tackle the overarching issues that seem beyond the capacity of committees to resolve. So bipartisan committees such as Armed Services, Agriculture, and Intelligence are usually able to process routine authorization bills. On issues for which there is no consensus, such as budgetary matters, which are a surrogate for the big government versus small government conflict, compromises have to be reached that can succeed on the Senate floor. This requires a collection of senators more diverse than the membership of a committee.

Another reason why gangs materialize is because of the inability of party leaders to produce compromise legislation. By their very nature, party leaders are polarizing figures, and their prominent involvement would jeopardize the chances of getting broad support for a bill. Conversely, as we have seen, party leaders look warily on bipartisan bills and amendments that might not win the favor of most senators in their caucus or give political cover to an opposition senator.

It may seem an obvious point, but moderate senators are much more likely both to initiate gangs and to join them than more ideologically rigid senators. The "moderation" of these senators may not necessarily be reflected in their voting records but in their disposition to do business with senators of the opposing party.

The manner in which the gangs form provides a window into the sometimes-inscrutable way that senators interact with each other. The most obvious connection between them, as we have seen, is being members of the same committee. Often, however, common membership does not appear to be an important factor. They can develop out of the most casual contact in any number of Senate venues, such encounters as in the Senate gymnasium or as members of CODELs (congressional delegation trips). Because their numbers are so small, it is easy for a senator to gauge the reputation of a colleague and the likelihood that he or she might become a legislative partner.

Senator Mark Warner (D-VA) recalled, "one of the best relationships I've had was not connected to any of the committees. It is with Saxby Chambliss (R-GA). That started with a conversation on the floor. The other traditional way people build relationships is through CODELs. When you're spending umpteen hours flying to Asia or Africa, you spend a lot of time with someone."[22]

Warner also remarked that that "there is some self-selection.... There are some folks that just view the world through an ideological prism and those who may have equally strong views but they also know that getting something done is important."[23]

Amity at the Alibi

Mark Warner is the senator who has gone further than anyone to promote relationships across party lines in the US Senate. A Virginia Democrat, Warner sees himself as being uniquely situated to bring colleagues together outside the walls of the Capitol. Coming from a swing state adjacent to Washington, DC, and having a home in nearby Alexandria, Warner explained, "I had the luxury others didn't have. I didn't have to spend two days a week commuting, which constrains your time and ... I had been lucky enough to have done well in business before I got here that I had both the resources and the settings, so I had the opportunities to do this that other members didn't have."

Since he arrived in the Senate in 2009, Warner has held a total of seventy-six meetings, retreats, and dinners at various places in the DC area that bring together Democrats and Republicans, including three "no agenda" dinners at the Alibi Club and one bipartisan dinner at his home in Alexandria. All told, Warner's bipartisan gatherings between 2011 and 2013 involved forty-seven senators, almost half of the membership of the Senate. In addition, Warner has been a member of three different "gangs": of Five (deficit), of Six (revenues and entitlements), and of Eight (immigration reform).

So how did Warner pick the forty-six senators who would receive invitations? I put that question to Warner and told him that I would probably have put together a list very similar to his based on what I know about the membership of the US Senate. He replied that there were people in the Senate whose careers "have been pretty much about being against stuff." The implication was that such senators were unlikely to be high on his list of invitees.

In a legislative body as small as the Senate and one that is under constant scrutiny by the media, reputations develop early in a senator's term. Senators don't necessarily accept the opinions of journalists or other outside observers without testing the relationship personally. More than three decades ago, a Democratic senator from the Midwest explained how the process worked for him:

> I go to the floor and I really don't know an issue. I know who does know it and who I trust and respect. You learn that. There are a number of people I wouldn't bother going to. They're a little sloppy or, you know, they may have a strong bias and not give you both sides.... You learn who's really qualified, who's really prepared, and who has really evaluated the situation.... You soon find out who among your colleagues is really reliable, has studied something in depth, and has a good, balanced view of things.[24]

Gang Busters? Party Leaders and Bipartisanship

People concerned about the political polarization in American life look upon any evidence of bipartisan cooperation like a traveler discovering an oasis in the desert. Journalists in the "mainstream media" constitute a kind of cheering section when any evidence of congressional bipartisanship shows up on their radar screen.[25] Within Congress itself, there is a group of individuals who are not natural allies of bipartisanship: the party leaders.

Nebraska Republican Mike Johanns mused on how his pledge to be bipartisan would probably disqualify him for a party leadership post:

> You know, if I walked into a caucus meeting and there was an election that day and I decided to run for conference chair and here's my message: "I am going to reach out and work with the Democrats and see what bills I can associate with them," I think they'd look at me and say, "Jeez, Mike, excuse me, what did you say?" I don't think you get elected to those positions if you have a kind of compromising personality.[26]

One of the responsibilities of party leaders is to minimize divisions within the ranks of their party. Bipartisan agreements, as we have seen, can place party leaders in the position of scuttling worthy bipartisan initiatives if they give too much to the other side. Bipartisan proposals, whether they originate in committees or as the result of ad hoc "gangs" of senators, often present a challenge to those whose responsibility is to safeguard party principles and increase, or at least maintain, the number of seats their party occupies.

A proposal that diluted, or worse, abandoned fundamentals of party doctrine, would be unwelcome to a party leader and to the various interest groups associated with the national parties. Leaders have a keen sense of the limits of bipartisanship and cast a wary eye on members of their party who seem to be bartering away cherished principles to get a deal that will win votes on the other side of the aisle.

Even more important from a tactical perspective is when party leaders confront a bipartisan initiative by one of their own senators that appears to give political cover to a senator of the opposing party. In the close-run contest for seats in the

Senate, bipartisanship is a luxury in which party leaders cannot indulge, especially when it involves giving cover to an opposition senator who is up for reelection in a state where a reputation for bipartisanship is politically useful.

When a party leader is up for reelection, the embrace of a bipartisan proposal by members of the leader's own party can create headaches. Up for reelection in 2014, Republican Senate Leader Mitch McConnell became concerned about the composition of the group of pro-immigration reform senators known as the Gang of Eight. If the bill that the gang produced was too heavily influenced by the four Democrats in the gang, it would create reelection problems for McConnell in Kentucky, a very conservative state where comprehensive immigration reform was unpopular. Accordingly, McConnell told John McCain, one of the Gang of Eight members, to include two conservative Republicans known to be critical of comprehensive immigration reform, Senators John Cornyn of Texas and Charles Grassley of Iowa. But "McCain thought the directive suggested that McConnell was trying to stifle the initiative. McCain ignored him and excluded Grassley and Cornyn from the group."[27]

The most well-intentioned bipartisanship also caused problems on the Democratic side. In 2011, Democrat Mark Warner announced that his bipartisan Gang of Six was "very close to a deal to reduce the federal deficit." Warner expressed the belief that everything had to be "on the table." That included "making Social Security more sustainable." What those statements implied was the possibility of raising the age of eligibility for Social Security recipients and the possibility of using a new way to index cost-of-living increases for current beneficiaries that would result in smaller increases. These proposals ran headlong into an oft-repeated pledge by Democratic Leader Harry Reid that Social Security should not be touched as part of any deal.[28]

When party leaders sense that a committee is either not acting swiftly enough on a piece of legislation or is about to produce legislation that departs significantly from core elements of party policy, they can simply swoop in and move the bill to the floor. Party leaders have also been involved in negotiating important pieces of legislation. "In 2007, for example, Majority Leader Harry Reid and Minority Leader Mitch McConnell negotiated a bipartisan deal on lobbying reform legislation—an issue that impacts members so directly [that] intensive leadership involvement [was] likely to be necessary."[29]

Bypassing committees by party leaders was the most frequently cited reason for polarization on the Senate floor by the senators I interviewed. For them, the "regular order" that prevails when committees are able to process legislation from the earliest point of holding hearings to the ultimate issuance of a committee report on a bipartisan vote greatly improves the likelihood that the bill will have bipartisan support when the bill reaches the floor. Republican senators were especially harsh in their comments about legislation brought to the floor by Majority Leader Reid that bypassed regular order.

Idaho Republican Mike Crapo recalled the fight over Obamacare that took place in the Senate Finance Committee: "That didn't even come out of the committee on a party-line vote. We tried to do a bipartisan deal, but then what was announced was that the bipartisan deal wasn't going to work because we were continuing to demand that there not be a single-payer system included, and the bill was actually written in the majority leader's office."[30]

Sometimes, leaders bypass committees for reasons that have nothing to do with fear that the legislation is being diluted by too much committee bipartisanship. On very important legislation or bills that fall under the jurisdiction of multiple committees, leaders may conclude that having it written by their staff would produce bills that were more timely and less complex.

Senate rules also forbid one committee to report out matters that lie within another committee's jurisdiction,[31] so it falls to the majority leader to assemble the products of various committees in order to produce a bill that reflects the preferences of all the committees involved.

There are times, however, when outside forces combine to prod Senate leadership to embrace bipartisanship. Occasionally, it involves something important, such as the agreement late in 2013 by members of a House-Senate conference committee to produce a budget, something that had not been done in almost three years. There are other circumstances in which dissatisfaction with Washington politics puts Congress on notice that it needs to do something—anything—that is bipartisan.

It is at such times that Congress reaches out, desperate for new legislation—or even old legislation that had languished—that can be presented as bipartisan. This can prove both dangerous and embarrassing for Congress. To paraphrase a French epigram originally applied to an impulsive marriage, "Legislate in haste, repent at leisure."

4

TENSIONS OVER BIPARTISANSHIP

LEADERS VERSUS COMMITTEES

In the previous chapter, I presented evidence of the considerable amount of bipartisanship on Senate committees and noted that when a bipartisan bill exits a committee, it encounters an environment less hospitable to bipartisanship. For one thing, the bill becomes the responsibility of party leaders whose strategies are influential, even decisive, in determining a bill's fate. And although the hand of committee chairs is not absent, since they are typically "floor managers" of a bill, their interests and those of their party leaders are by no means congruent.

Committee chairmen and party leaders often see the world very differently. Committee chairmen, as we have seen, have a proprietary attitude toward their committees and want to preserve their jurisdiction and autonomy. Quality of life is also important to them, and maintaining a good relationship with the ranking member of the other party makes for a more harmonious committee. They may also develop a sensitivity to the views of the opposing party because of their continuous interaction at close hand. Committee members are also attuned to the needs and concerns of the external constituencies that are the clients of their committee—something they share with their colleagues in the opposing party.

Committees stand at the apex of what have been called "iron triangles," "subgovernments," and "policy domains."[1] As such, committees have been characterized as "outliers," that certain committees are not representative of the chamber as a whole. It was suggested that the two Armed Services Committees, for example, have memberships considerably more conservative than the House and Senate as a whole, and that other committees might be atypically liberal.[2] This picture of ideologically atypical committees sets a lively debate among political scientists, some of whom subscribe to the belief that committees are, in a way, ideologically deviant and others who see them as reasonable reflections of the larger body.[3]

Committees of Congress may or may not be ideologically anomalous, but they are certainly distinctive in their jurisdictions and distinguishable from one another in the level of partisanship or bipartisanship that prevails at any given time. Their distinctiveness extends to the committee's solidarity in the face of countervailing pressure that typically comes from party leadership and the party caucuses on whose behalf the leaders act.

Party leaders, especially the majority leader, approach things with a very different set of political needs. This is especially true if the president is of the leader's party and the leader has the responsibility to advance the president's agenda as well as that of the party caucus of which the leader is, in a sense, the trustee. More than that, the majority leader also represents the party at large, especially the base, who are its most passionate and ideological citizen supporters. Nonetheless, party leaders understand the value of bipartisanship both in terms of promoting legislative success and also as a positive message to the elector-ate. Accordingly, party leaders can find themselves faced with the Solomonic challenge of trying to pursue a bipartisan course favored by a committee without betraying fundamental party principles dear to the party's caucus and citizen supporters. The campaign for healthcare reform in 2009 involved such tensions.

Straining for Bipartisanship: The Baucus Caucus

Relations between Senator Max Baucus, chairman of the Sen-ate Finance Committee, and his party's leader, Senator Tom Daschle, had been contentious. Daschle, who served as a Demo-cratic leader from 1994 until he was defeated for reelection in 2004, involved himself actively, sometimes intrusively, in the business of the committees. This hands-on approach did not sit well with the chairmen, especially Senator Baucus, who was fiercely defensive of his committee and of his relationship with his ranking member, Senator Chuck Grassley (R-IA). A former Republican colleague of Baucus (a centrist in a party that leaned left), said, "Max has always made some Democrats nervous."[4]

After Daschle's defeat in 2004, Baucus found in Daschle's successor, Harry Reid, a more congenial leader. Reid took a more laissez-faire approach, did not involve himself in the details of committee work, and gave his committee chairs a free hand.

In 2009, Baucus was to play a central role in the enactment of the Patient Protection and Affordable Care Act (Obamacare) by reason of jurisdiction of his committee, which his commit-tee shared with other Senate panels, principal among them the Committee on Health, Education, Labor, and Pensions. The HELP Committee, as it is known, was quite a different com-mittee from Finance. Its long-time chairman had been Senator Edward M. Kennedy (D-MA), a prominent liberal. When Ken-nedy became ill with brain cancer, Senator Christopher Dodd (D-CT) took over as acting chairman. The Republicans on the

HELP Committee were a bit less conservative than those on Finance. Nonetheless, the effort to secure bipartisan support was more serious on the Finance Committee than on HELP.

Because so many of the healthcare reform proposals involved taxation and spending, the Finance Committee acted as a kind of funnel for almost all of the proposals connected with the plan, so all eyes were on chairman Max Baucus and the committee's ranking member, Charles Grassley. The two senators had an unusually close relationship—too close in the eyes of many of Baucus's Democratic colleagues. They feared that the chairman, in the interest of bringing Grassley along on a health reform bill and endowing it with bipartisanship, would grant the Republican too much influence in shaping the bill and, consequently, produce legislation too conservative to be acceptable to the Democratic leadership and the party caucus as a whole. Within the Finance Committee itself, an informal bipartisan Gang of Six that included Baucus and Grassley worked on a compromise bill throughout the late spring and early summer of 2009.[5]

With the August recess, senators went home, held town meetings, and were quickly besieged by constituents who either favored the healthcare reform or opposed it. In his town meetings in Iowa, Grassley heard from both sides, but what troubled him the most was the negative reaction from Republican voters. At a town meeting in Winterset, Iowa, Grassley seemed chastened by the hostility to the healthcare bill and began to sound his retreat from it. "Nothing may come out of our committee," Grassley said. "It may not be something I can agree with, so I may be pushed away from the table."[6]

As his trip across Iowa progressed, Grassley became acutely aware that a storm was brewing on the right and began to fear that he would be challenged in a Republican primary by someone far more conservative and that he would be attacked for being associated with healthcare reform. Accordingly, his statements on reform became increasingly negative, especially those made to potential contributors to his campaign. In his fund-raising letter, Grassley said, "I had to rush you this Air-Gram today to set the record straight on my firm and unwavering opposition to government-run healthcare and ask your immediate support in helping me defeat Obamacare."[7]

By September, it was clear that no acceptable compromise would be coming from the Gang of Six on the Finance Committee. "The group of Senate Finance Committee members has, instead, proved a time-sucking bust, with no compromise after months of negotiations and plenty of Senate Democrats peeved at the influence ceded to the gang's GOP members."[8] The delay caused by Baucus's efforts to develop bipartisanship was a source of concern to the Democratic leadership, and he was given a deadline to produce a bill.

Baucus's objective for "meaningful bipartisan legislation that can pass the Senate and become law this year," however, proved to be elusive. "Such pragmatism can make more liberal Democrats nervous and has drawn the ire of fellow Democrats."[9]

As appealing as the idea of a bipartisan healthcare reform bill was, a bill acceptable to Grassley would likely be rejected out of hand by Baucus's fellow Democratic colleagues. But not all committee Republicans were out of reach, and Baucus shifted his focus away from Grassley and in the direction of Maine senator Olympia Snowe, whose endorsement of the bill would endow it with at least token bipartisanship. The price Baucus had to pay for bipartisanship was to drop the provision most passionately sought by members of the party's progressive wing: a government-sponsored health insurance plan to compete with private insurers. The Democratic majority in the House had endorsed the "public option," as had the HELP Committee.

But the importance to both Baucus and President Obama of giving at least a shade of bipartisanship to health reform legislation induced both men to accommodate Senator Snowe, for whom "simply inserting a government-sponsored plan into the dysfunctional insurance marketplace wasn't a panacea for the problems of obtaining health coverage."[10] But Snowe's vote in favor of the legislation on October 13, 2009, was discounted by her fellow Republicans because of her history of cooperation across party lines. On the other hand, "Snowe's buy-in could make it easier for Baucus and Reid to sell reform to moderate Democrats ... who are arguably more conservative than their colleague from Maine."[11]

It now fell to Majority Leader Reid to harmonize the Finance Committee bill, with its mild bipartisan coloration, with the HELP Committee bill that had passed without any Republican votes. Snowe, whose vote in the committee was so eagerly solicited by the Democratic leadership and the White House, made no promises that she would vote for the final product. Indeed, over the course of the next six weeks, when it became apparent that the bill could be passed with the votes of the Senate's sixty Democrats, the price of accommodating Snowe's concerns was seen by Reid as too steep. Better to lose a single dissatisfied Republican whose ultimate support was not assured than to alienate Democrats who objected to her conditions.

The Price of Bipartisanship

From the perspective of a party leader in the Senate, what is bipartisan is not necessarily good and what is good is not necessarily bipartisan, even though it is so widely praised as the alternative to the gridlock in American politics. Flexibility can be seen as appeasement or worse: betrayal of core principles and constituencies to which leaders need to be attuned. It may just not be possible to "get to yes" without producing legislation that is so insipid and watered-down that it fails to deal with the problem it was designed to address. Neither, however, does forcing great legislative innovations on slender majorities produce wholly satisfactory results, as we have seen with Obamacare, which passed in 2009 with no Republican support and was later resisted fiercely in the Republican-controlled House of Representatives, which voted more than forty times to repeal it.

Party Leaders versus Bipartisanship

On election day 2010, the Democrats took what President Obama called "a shellacking." They lost their majority in the House of Representatives but managed to retain control of the Senate. Opposition to what came to be known as "Obamacare" was widely blamed for the party's losses.

The retention of the Senate majority by the Democrats was, however, tenuous. At the end of 2011, the Senate had fifty-one Democrats, two independents who caucused with them, and forty-seven Republicans. The prospects for Democrats in 2012 looked gloomy. Twenty-one Democrats were up for reelection and only ten Republicans. Moreover, six incumbent Democratic senators had announced that they would not be seeking new terms, including those in North Dakota and Nebraska, which were thought to be easy pick-ups for Republicans.

A majority leader without a majority is called a minority leader, and Harry Reid, the majority leader and a shrewd and tough politician, had no intention of losing his majority. Reid's self-imposed goal in 2012 was to preserve his majority. Much of what he did that year can be explained by that objective. It would compel him, on more than one occasion, to oppose bipartisan initiatives that might have conflicted with that goal. One such bipartisan initiative involved one of the few pieces of legislation to pass the 112th Congress, the STOCK Act.

In response to a segment on the CBS news program *60 Minutes* and a plea from President Obama in his State of the Union speech to bar members of Congress from using their knowledge to make stock purchases, the Senate took up the

STOCK Act. Some members of the Senate were dismissive of the bill, but it was thought to be a measure that might be able to pass a badly polarized Congress. Senators flocked to offer amendments to the bill designed to toughen its terms. One bipartisan amendment came from Democrat Kirsten Gillibrand of New York and Republican Scott Brown of Massachusetts.

In a special election in 2009, Scott Brown had won the Senate seat held for many years by Senator Edward Kennedy. The election was a serious setback for the Democrats not only because it deprived them of the sixtieth vote to end filibusters, but because it took the seat of one of the party's legendary figures in a strongly Democratic state. The Democrats vowed to reclaim the seat in 2012 and found a challenger to Brown in Elizabeth Warren, a Harvard Law professor and a consumer activist. A bipartisan amendment would, of course, give Brown political cover by ingratiating him with Massachusetts Democrats, whose votes he would need to win a full term in the Senate, something that Democratic Leader Reid could hardly support.

As leader, Reid had several options to derail the Gillibrand-Brown amendment. The one he selected was an amendment that he himself would offer, known as a "side-by-side amendment," that closely resembled the bipartisan amendment and could draw away support from Gillibrand-Brown. This is illustrative of the enormous influence the majority leader enjoys in the amendment process. He can also, by reason of the fact that he is recognized first by the presiding officer in the Senate, "fill the amendment tree" by offering amendments that take up all available spots allowed under the rules.

Reid also sought to protect those Democrats facing reelection in 2012 by stating that a budget resolution was unnecessary in light of the Budget Control Act of 2011. The resolution gives rise to a riotous process known on Capitol Hill as "vote-a-rama," a stage in the budget process when senators flock to offer amendments to budget legislation that senators regard as a "vehicle." As Senator Mark Warner noted in the previous chapter, vote-a-rama is also used to introduce amendments calculated to force members of the opposition party to go on record on controversial matters.

On the Republican side, leaders' protective attitude toward vulnerable GOP senators could be seen in a bill to pay for the notorious "bridge to nowhere" that connects the town of Ketchikan, Alaska, with Gravina Island, where the town's airport is located. Oklahoma Republican Tom Coburn opposed the project because of its hefty price tag and the fact that Gravina Island had only fifty residents.[12]

The bridge's sponsor in the Senate was Coburn's fellow Republican Senator Ted Stevens from Alaska, who was deeply committed to the project and not a man to be crossed by senators of either party, as he was chairman of the powerful Appropriations Committee.

Coburn proposed an amendment to delete the funds for the bridge and direct them to road work in Louisiana, a state recovering from Hurricane Katrina. Coburn described the reaction to his amendment:

> I put an amendment on the "bridge to nowhere." All the Republicans didn't want me to put that amendment on it. They could have objected. They didn't. They hated the amendment. The vast majority of them didn't vote for the amendment, but I got the amendment and the (Republican) Majority Leader [Bill Frist] said, "Oh no, this is too hard a vote for our guys. I don't want them to vote on this." So only fifteen people voted with me and we lost.[13]

When leaders perceive bipartisanship as a source of political peril for members of their caucus, they will act forcefully to squelch it. By nature of their jobs, leaders are trained to perceive the danger lurking behind the benign façade of amendments that enjoy the support from both parties as if it were poisoned bait.[14] Leaders, the guardians of partisan majorities, extol the virtues of bipartisan measures while at the same time being wary of the snares that lurk within. Committee members, especially ranking members, will for their part embrace bipartisanship to protect the turf of their committees even at the risk of clashing with their party's leadership.

Such was the case in the aftermath of the decision by Majority Leader Harry Reid in December 2013 to curtail the use of the filibuster in Senate rules so as to enable executive branch nominees to be confirmed by a simple majority. Republicans reacted angrily, and none more so than Minority Leader Mitch McConnell, who vowed to use any procedural device available to him to thwart Reid.[15]

McConnell's first target was the defense authorization bill that Reid wanted to be adopted without Republican amendments, a practice, as we have seen, which was deeply resented by the GOP minority. The ranking Republican on the Armed Services Committee, James Inhofe of Oklahoma, was no less distressed by the absence of amendments than were his fellow Republicans, but he put his role "as ranking Republican on the Senate Armed Services Committee above any efforts to stymie Reid."[16]

For Inhofe, passage of the bill was a matter of personal pride and committee tradition. Inhofe joined with committee chairman Carl Levin to make the case that the Armed Services Committee had managed to pass the bill out of committee for the past fifty-one years. Inhofe stressed the unique features of the bill: "The defense bill is different than all other bills. It's the one bill that you have to give the resources to our kids who are fighting battles, and so it has to be treated differently. That has to have priority over process."[17]

For most Republicans, the absence of amendments condemned the bill because an unamended bill would represent a victory for Majority Leader Reid and a vindication of his practice of blocking Republican amendments that might be seen as difficult votes for Democrats.

The reaction of committee Republicans added weight to the belief that Armed Services was indeed an outlier, when other committee Republicans rallied to Inhofe and, not incidentally, to the committee Democratic chairman Carl Levin. The first of these Republicans was the man Inhofe replaced as ranking Republican member, John McCain, who "provided key backup for Inhofe by vocally supporting the compromise bill and lobbying Republican colleagues."[18]

Inhofe brought the proposal to pass the bill without amendments to the Republican caucus meeting, where Minority Leader Mitch McConnell and a number of other Republican senators—none of whom were members of the Armed Services Committee—attacked the plan. But McCain's art of persuasion worked on two Republican senators who were on Armed Services, Roger Wicker of Mississippi and Kelly Ayotte of New Hampshire. Their votes were needed to invoke cloture because the bill had a 60-vote threshold to terminate debate and proceed to a vote.[19] Despite his objections, McConnell ultimately supported moving ahead to a vote.

Lacking the instruments of procedural control available to Reid, McConnell was forced to back down in the face of a strong push by Democratic and Republican members of the Armed Services Committee. So while Reid was able to quash the bipartisan Gillibrand-Brown amendment, McConnell was forced to accept defeat at the hands of a strong bipartisan majority. What differentiates the two cases, besides the superior procedural tools wielded by Reid, is that the majority leader faced down a pair of senators, not the solid opposition of a committee led by its ranking members.

Flickers of Bipartisanship

As we have seen in this chapter, bipartisanship in the Senate can survive, even thrive, but its vitality depends on a number of conditions that are not always present. The opposition of the majority leader is almost always fatal; the minority leader much less so. A particularly strong bipartisan coalition on a committee may carry the day, but it must certainly include the committee's most senior members.

The substance of the legislation in question is crucial. It is important to recognize that the success of the leadership of the Armed Services Committee in blunting the opposition of Senator McConnell has much to do with the broad support enjoyed by the military in the public and, by extension, in Congress.

Moreover, the defense authorization bill, like the agriculture bill, tends not to be ideologically divisive, unlike the Affordable Care Act in the Finance Committee. Differences over the effectiveness of weapons systems resembles the arguments over agricultural commodities and may reflect the presence of major defense contractors or military bases in a senator's state rather than deeply held geo-strategic philosophies. With its jurisdiction over taxation, the Finance Committee stands at the very fault line of American politics: the appropriate size, cost, and scope of federal government. And while Finance has historically enjoyed great prestige because of its jurisdiction, it was not able to surmount the polarizing issues that were handed it.

Senator Tom Coburn gave up his seat on the committee because

> Finance didn't do anything. I didn't want to waste my time being on a committee that didn't accomplish anything.... If you think about the fact that the biggest problem facing our country is that Medicare is crashing from a demographic standpoint and a cost standpoint and that Social Security is insolvent and will be out of

money in thirteen months, all the time I was on that committee—three full years—we did not address one of those three major issues.[20]

Healthcare reform is just too political an issue around which to form a consensus, even with a committee leadership inclined to work in bipartisan harmony.

5
COSMETIC BIPARTISANSHIP?

Much activity on Capitol Hill in the age of political polarization has less to do with legislation than with messaging. It has always been true, of course, that few bills introduced in the course of a two-year Congress make it into law, but in a polarized political environment and divided government, where the prospects of enactments are even slimmer, bills are often introduced by senators and representatives who know their bill will never see a presidential signature but who hope that the bill will be good messaging material.

Political messaging has several objectives. One is to express solidarity with the political base of one's party. The repeated efforts by House Republicans to repeal Obamacare is an example of messaging to a portion of their party's base for whom the healthcare reform legislation is odious. In the certain knowledge that such repeal efforts would never pass the Senate, these bills are the purest form of messaging to the base.

There is also messaging designed to embarrass the opposing party. Congressional Democrats in 2012 embroidered the message that the Republicans were "antiwoman" to the point where it became an elaborate narrative that paradoxically was occasionally abetted by Republican candidates themselves, who offered bizarre views of rape and female anatomy.

But both parties embrace yet another form of messaging when suffering from low public approval: bipartisan messaging. This is a signal sent to convey the impression that all is not lost on Capitol Hill, that Democrats and Republicans can unite to achieve some worthy goal.

Bipartisanship may not be fully understood by all parts of the electorate, but it is by no means of negligible political value to politicians who see it as a useful badge. Endowing legislation with bipartisan parentage is especially valuable if a bill introduced in Congress has a reasonable hope of passage. The cosmetic value of such legislation is usually far out of proportion to its substantive importance. In the 112th Congress, two examples stand out: the STOCK Act and the JOBS Act.

In the previous chapter, the STOCK Act of 2012 was cited as an example of the problem faced by a Democratic leader by a bipartisan amendment that would have benefitted a Republican senator who was up for reelection. The STOCK Act was the product of an urge to appear both productive and bipartisan at a time of low approval ratings for both parties in Congress.

No less affected by the urge was President Obama, who was hoping to regain public support after an electoral humiliation for his party that he accepted as a personal repudiation. This desire for collective redemption produced two bills, both of which were quickly passed by both houses of Congress with strong bipartisan majorities and signed by President Obama. Within little more than a year, major portions of one of these acts had been repealed. The other yielded few political dividends to the president and his party in Congress and may even have opened the door to fraud in the marketing of the initial public offerings of Internet-related securities.

Taking Stock of the STOCK Act

Congress loves bills whose subject matter can be fashioned into catchy acronyms, and the STOCK Act (Stop Trading on Congressional Knowledge) was an outstanding example. The bill had first been introduced in the House in 2006, but it languished there, attracting few cosponsors and no media attention. But on November 18, 2011, the most widely watched news program on television, *60 Minutes*, ran a story presented by one of its senior correspondents, Steve Kroft, who reported that members of Congress had been making investments based on information gained as part of their official duties. Kroft singled out two of Congress's most visible members, House Speaker John Boehner and House Minority Leader Nancy Pelosi.

Much of the information used by *60 Minutes* came from a book by conservative author Peter Schweizer entitled *Throw Them All Out*. The report on *60 Minutes* came at a time when Congress's approval rating in the polls was less than 20 percent.[1] Obama was still reeling from the beating his party had suffered in the 2010 election and from his failure to come to an agreement with House Speaker Boehner on a "grand bargain" to deal with the federal deficit and tax reform. It was a rare moment in which the interests of the ideological combatants of the capital could converge, and they reasoned that they could patch up their reputations with bipartisan legislation that imposed harsh controls on the investments of members of Congress.

In its original form, the STOCK Act required that members of Congress and congressional staff members whose annual salary was more than $118,000 disclose their assets, liabilities (such as home mortgages), and financial transactions worth more than $1,000 and have the information posted on a downloadable online database. This information would presumably allow visitors to the site to ascertain whether members of Congress or their staff members were working on legislation in which they had a financial stake.

In his State of the Union message on January 14, 2012, President Obama said, "Send me a bill that bans insider trading by members of Congress and I will sign it tomorrow." Although it was neither sent nor signed the next day, it was launched on a fast track to passage.

Majority Leader Reid and Republican Minority Leader McConnell had agreed between themselves that they would support a narrowly focused STOCK bill that outlawed trading by members and staff using inside information. That meeting of the minds was brief because the ranking Republican member of the Banking Committee, Richard Shelby of Alabama, demanded an amendment that high officials of the executive branch also be forced to disclose their stock holdings and financial transactions. Broadening the bill beyond Congress would ultimately prove to be the unraveling of the STOCK Act.

But for the present, the prospect of support by both party leaders signaled that the bill was a legislative "vehicle" that would likely pass the Senate. This realization set the stage for a vote-a-rama, a torrent of amendments, most of which were offered by junior senators who vied with each other to demonstrate to the American people how much pain the Senate could inflict on itself. These pageants of congressional masochism occur from time to time when senators and House members see their approval ratings sinking to abysmal levels and feel the need for self-abasement.

On January 31, 2012, Senator Rand Paul, a Kentucky Republican, topped the scales of punitive amendments by imposing a lifetime ban on retired members of Congress from becoming lobbyists, a common career choice after members retire. A number of Senator Paul's colleagues had announced plans to retire at the end of the 112th Congress and were furious at this amendment from a very junior colleague, especially since some of them were headed "downtown" to become lobbyists. Even those senators who were not retiring took the floor to condemn Paul's amendment. Senator Susan Collins, a fellow Republican, questioned whether his amendment, if enacted, would even be constitutional. Democratic Whip Dick Durbin accused Paul of harassing members in their retirement. On February 2, after being offered the opportunity to offer three other amendments by the majority leader, Paul withdrew his amendment.[2]

In the House of Representatives, the groundwork had already been laid by the bill that had been introduced in 2006 that covered only members of Congress. As in the Senate, the legislation enjoyed strong bipartisan support, and on April 4, 2012, President Obama signed the STOCK Act into law. Compared to the glacial pace of most legislation, the STOCK Act's path to enactment was positively supersonic.

Doubling Down on Bipartisanship: The JOBS Bill

At roughly the same time that the STOCK Act was under discussion, another piece of legislation labeled with an equally appealing acronym was introduced in the House; the JOBS (Jumpstart Our Business Startups) Act. On March 19, 2012, the House passed the bill with a strong bipartisan vote and the endorsement of President Obama.

The stated purpose of the JOBS bill was to simplify the process for new companies to gain access to capital markets and to lower the cost to the startup companies of complying with securities regulations. The bill also facilitated "crowd funding," raising money from investors online. This latter provision rang alarm bells in the minds of some Senate Democrats, who claimed that the loosened regulations ran the risk of defrauding investors by allowing the companies to avoid publicly disclosing important financial information.[3]

While the Obama administration approved of the STOCK
Act, it could not claim authorship. The JOBS Act, in contrast,
came about because of a series of decisions made by the White
House after the disastrous 2010 congressional election. They
were designed to portray the Obama administration as friendly
to the business community. This was, in part, to repair a relationship that was never very close but was made worse when
the administration embraced the Dodd-Frank legislation that
imposed restrictions on the financial services industry because
of its role in the 2008 recession.

To improve the ties to the business community, the president
brought to the White House a politically prominent banker
as chief of staff, William M. Daley. The White House also
established a Jobs and Competitiveness Council chaired by the
CEO of General Electric, Jeffrey Immelt, and included members from the business community. In addition, the Treasury
Department set up a task force to explore ways that companies
could raise money from investors. The president also ordered
a review of regulations to see which were excessively burden-
some to business.

It is possible that President Obama was unaware of some
of the details of the bill and that if he had looked into it
more closely he might have concluded that the bill was "too
Republican" and would cause problems both for Democrats in
Congress and liberal interest groups. Nonetheless, the bless-
ing of the president was a powerful incentive for congressional
Democrats to follow suit.

Democratic Leader Reid quickly found himself in an awk-
ward position: a White House committee established by a Democratic president had authored a bill that was quickly embraced
by congressional Republicans. Its appearance, however, quickly
sounded alarm bells with liberal groups and a substantial number of Democratic senators who were wary of features of a bill
that seemed to leave consumers vulnerable to fraud.

The president's endorsement and the Republicans' embrace
of the bill made it a tough bill to oppose or even to modify if a

robust signal of bipartisanship was to be sent. Boxed in on the one hand by the president and on the other by House Republicans, the Senate Democratic leadership scrambled to fashion an alternative bill more palatable to Democrats.

Had the president not embraced the bill so enthusiastically and unreservedly, the Senate Democrats might have been able to use the threat of a veto to bargain with the Republicans for a more acceptable bill. As it was, the president could hardly threaten to veto a bill he had so enthusiastically endorsed. The immediate effect of the bill in the Senate was to split the Democratic caucus.

Majority Leader Reid's lack of enthusiasm for the bill could hardly have been more obvious. He could not even bear to refer to it as the JOBS bill, preferring instead to call it "the IPO bill" because it promised to "make it easier for financiers and their clients in the technology industry to raise money for their companies' operations through the use of initial public offerings."[4] The White House proceeded to muster all of its resources to press for Senate passage. In the words of one staff member, "The White House worked the caucus hard and even brought Barney Frank in to push it as well."[5] (Frank was the co-author of the Dodd-Frank financial services reform bill popular with liberals.)

Labor unions, among the most loyal elements in the Democratic political base, were especially hostile to the JOBS bill. Richard Trumka, president of the AFL-CIO, was so upset with the possibility that the JOBS Act might pass that he prevailed upon his executive council to issue a statement condemning Congress for "once again looking to deregulate Wall Street ... and weaken the ability of the Securities and Exchange Commission to regulate our capital markets and allow companies to sell stock to the public without ... adequate internal controls and without complying with key corporate governance reforms in the recently-passed Dodd-Frank Act."[6]

By the end of March 2012, a serious uprising among Senate Democrats was in progress, led by Michigan senator Carl

Levin and Oregon's Jeff Merkley. Deputy Majority Leader Dick Durbin spoke out against it on the floor of the Senate. With a vote on the bill scheduled for April 3, Reid convened a caucus meeting on Thursday, March 26, to head off a possible filibuster of the bill by members of his own party. The spectacle of Democratic senators filibustering a bill endorsed by a Democratic president was a nightmare for Reid. He reportedly warned his Democratic colleagues in the caucus meeting against blocking a vote on a bipartisan bill supported by the president. When the Senate finally voted to proceed with the bill, half of the Democratic senators voted against it.[7] When the final vote took place, the JOBS Act, having already passed the House, passed the Senate by a vote of 73–26, despite a desperate last-minute effort by Carl Levin to persuade his colleagues to kill it.

A Democratic staff member gave voice to the frustrations of many Democrats: "It is a lousy bill. The White House screwed up by endorsing it and taking away the possibility of a veto and stripping the [Senate] Democrats of any leverage."

In the course of a few weeks, the Senate, reviled for its lack of achievement, had managed to pass two bipartisan bills. On the face of it, it was a perfect positive-sum game. The president and both parties in Congress could claim bipartisan success, but the self-congratulation masked a less-charitable perspective beyond the public's view. When asked if the Senate could look back on the period of both the STOCK Act and the JOBS Act as one of great accomplishment, a senior Democratic staff member snapped, "Why, because we passed two lousy bills?"[8]

The STOCK Act: Act II

The signing of the STOCK Act was an occasion for bipartisan celebration. At the bill signing at the White House, the president proclaimed, "The powerful shouldn't get to create one set of rules for themselves and another set of rules for everybody else."

The General Services Administration picked up the $250,000 tab for the bill-signing pageant.[9] However, the celebratory spirit did not last long.

On July 19, 2012, CNN reported that the House and Senate had conflicting interpretations of the bill that they had just passed. The previous month, the Senate Ethics Committee released guidelines for those affected by the bill that said that stock trades of more than $1,000 had to be reported within forty-five days and that the reporting requirement included the trades of spouses and dependent children. The guidelines of the House Ethics Committee contained no such requirement for spouses and children. The Office of Government Ethics, the organization enforcing the STOCK Act in the executive branch, sided with the interpretation of the House committee.[10]

Within a week, the STOCK Act came under attack for another provision in the bill that no one in Congress seemed to have anticipated. On July 26, fourteen former officials of the intelligence community wrote a letter to Congress stating that the STOCK Act's requirement that financial information be posted online "would be a jackpot for enemies of the United States intent on finding security vulnerabilities they can exploit."[11]

Privacy concerns also surrounded the posting of the financial reports. Unions representing employees of the Congressional Research Service, Social Security Administration law judges, and immigration judges objected to the law as "a serious threat to the safety and security [of employees], not to mention the unwarranted invasion of their privacy."[12]

The reporting requirements of the STOCK Act gave rise to nightmarish speculations. Suppose a staff member's parents gave a gift of stock to the staff member's child? Under the Senate interpretation, the minor child's name and address would need to be posted and could be downloaded by sex offenders.

Despite all of these potential dangers, the House moved quickly to bring its interpretation in line with that of the Senate.

On a voice vote (not a recorded vote, in which each member's vote is identified) on September 27, 2012, the House passed legislation delaying until December 8 the requirement that all affected individuals post their information online.[13]

Almost simultaneously, the Senate passed a similar bill delaying implementation of the act. This bill said that the delay was meant "to prevent harm to the national security by endangering the military officers and civilian employees to whom the publication requirement applies."[14] But a lawsuit filed by a group of federal employees resulted in a US district court judge temporarily blocking the implementation of the law, noting that the law violated federal workers' rights to privacy by requiring them to disclose their financial information.

When the December deadline approached, Congress delayed the implementation once again. This delay was to allow a study commissioned by Congress to examine the possible security problems that the bill's posting requirements might pose. The study was conducted by the National Academy of Public Administration (NAPA), an organization that describes itself as "an independent, nonprofit, and non-partisan organization established to assist government leaders in building more effective, accountable, and transparent organizations.[15]

The STOCK Act: The Finale

On March 13, 2013, NAPA issued its report. The study concluded that "posting personal financial information as required by the act does indeed impose unwarranted risk to national security and law enforcement as well as threaten agency missions, individual safety, and privacy." It went on to recommend that Congress impose an indefinite delay in requiring the posting of personal financial information online.[16]

As celebratory as was the signing of the STOCK Act, its demise was muted. A month after the NAPA report was issued,

Congress quietly gutted the STOCK Act, removing the requirement for those covered by the act to enter their financial information in a searchable online database. A liberal online news site complained that "both chambers of Congress quickly—and almost silently—approved, by unanimous consent, the repeal legislation ... just before heading home to their districts. The Senate advanced the bill Thursday by unanimous consent, without debate or even briefly describing what it would do."[17]

Harsh criticism came from the other side of the political spectrum as well, but it was not a lament for the STOCK Act. Rather, it was an attack on the way Congress does business. Writing for the blog RedState, Daniel Horowitz reflected, "The broader point is how Congress can go from passing something with unanimous consent one year and repealing it by unanimous consent the following year—without any mea culpa."[18]

What remained of the STOCK Act after exempting employees of the executive branch and legislative staff from the requirement to post their finances online was the mandate to comply for the president, vice president, members of Congress, candidates for Congress, and a handful of individuals nominated by the president and subject to Senate confirmation. Reporting was still required, but anyone seeking the information could not get it online. The request would need to be made in person.

It also made insider trading by members of Congress illegal. This last thread of tattered legislation held perhaps the most supreme irony of this episode of Congress's ritual purification: that in the opinion of the Securities and Exchange Commission (SEC), the chief federal regulatory agency for American stock markets, insider trading by members of Congress had been illegal for many years. What Congress had been engaged in for over a year was, in the eyes of the SEC, a solution in search of a problem.[19]

This was a bill that was thought to be unnecessary even by many of those who worked on it. The committee of jurisdiction in the Senate was the Committee on Government Affairs and

Homeland Security, whose members expressed little interest in a bill they thought redundant. Ultimately, six Senate committees worked the bill. A jurisdictional objection by one of those committees—Senate Ethics—threatened at one point to kill the bill. Harry Reid remarked, "It was the worst bill ever." The STOCK Act was reduced to an ineffectual shadow of its former self, so arguably little actual harm had been done.

The JOBS Act was quite another thing. It came under immediate attack as a bill that would "very nearly legalize fraud in the stock market." Worse, "this law actually appears to have been specifically written to encourage fraud in the stock market."[20]

Two years after the passage of the JOBS Act, scorn and indignation continued to rain down on the law, Congress, and the SEC, the agency designated by Congress to set up the rules for the "crowd-funding" process that would make it easier to start high-tech companies.

In a top-of-the-page editorial, the *New York Times* declared:

> In an election year sop to special interests, Congress passed a law in 2012 to end or loosen many bedrock investor protections on the grounds that deregulation would make it easier for companies to raise money. Among the changes, the law, deceptively named the JOBS Act, called for the SEC to write rules to establish a crowd-funding marketplace, where companies could raise up to $1 million a year without having to meet disclosure and accounting standards that had long applied whenever private ventures raised money from the public. Perhaps the law's one and only saving grace was that it also required the SEC to place new safeguards against the heightened potential in crowd funding for big losses from fraudulent or unsuitable offerings.... But the SEC's proposed rules basically let intermediaries satisfy the antifraud obligation by relying on the companies' own representations.[21]

So why did Congress labor on it for eighteen months? On one level, it was an effort by Congress, often depicted as being out of touch, to identify with the IT companies seen as the beneficiaries of the law. The deeper motive was the collective fear on the part of members that the American public held them in disrepute and the collective hope that their reputations could be salvaged by a bipartisan gift to the technology community. But, in the end, it turned out to be political fool's gold.

If the desire for bipartisan camouflage results in Congress producing two bills of such dubious quality, one is prompted to question the value and importance of bipartisanship. These were two pieces of legislation whose narrowness and superficial lack of any ideological burden made them appealing to a gridlocked Senate. They were, however, poorly conceived and enacted in a virtual state of panic, especially the STOCK Act. The JOBS Act was a transparent effort on the part of Congress to ingratiate itself with "the next big thing."

But in the absence of agreement by the two parties on legislation of broader importance, would it make sense for Congress to shun bipartisan bills merely because they are not landmark legislation?

In the next chapter we will consider the question of whether Congress's time, in the absence of consensus on legislation of broad import, is fruitfully spent on bills of limited breadth that can pass simply because what recommends them most strongly is that they enjoy bipartisan support. We will also consider arguments made by critics from many places on the political spectrum that the search for bipartisanship is a chimerical quest actuated more by misguided nostalgia than by sound reason.

6
IS BIPARTISANSHIP DEAD?

On September 20, 2013, Rep. Kevin McCarthy, the House Republicans' deputy majority leader had an announcement to make after one of the forty-four times the House voted to repeal the Patient Protection and Affordable Care Act (Obamacare). Explaining the vote, McCarthy was quoted as saying, "It wasn't just a group of Republicans. It was a bipartisan vote." McCarthy urged the journalists in the room to make note of that fact. One reporter, Aaron Blake of the *Washington Post*, did just that and learned that the bill was indeed bipartisan, that is, if you define bipartisanship as a bill supported by 231 Republicans and 2 Democrats.[1]

What level of support from the opposing party qualifies a bill to be bipartisan? The budget resolution enacted in late 2013 was trumpeted as a conspicuous act of bipartisanship because nine Republican senators joined all fifty-three Democrats and two independents to pass it. In their headlines, the *Washington Post*, ABC News, the website of the National Education Association,

National Public Radio, and the World Socialist Website (albeit snidely) all used the adjective "bipartisan" to characterize the vote.[2] While that may not constitute a consensus on the bipartisan credentials of the budget agreement, it does suggest that at a time of stark polarization, nine votes may well meet the not-too-rigorous test.

Early in 2010, a $15 billion jobs bill drafted by Majority Leader Harry Reid succeeded in overcoming a Republican filibuster by a vote of 62–30. Five Republican senators supported Reid's motion to debate the bill. Getting to a final vote on the passage of the bill would have to weather several more hurdles, but just getting the bill debated on the floor of the Senate was described as "a rare bipartisan breakthrough."[3]

An article printed the same day in the *Washington Post* also characterized the procedural vote as "a breakthrough."[4] In the aftermath of the struggle over Obamacare, which received not a single Republican vote, a procedural vote of 62–30 on the $15 billion jobs bill—which was supported by five Republicans—clearly qualified as a bipartisan moment. But at least one media source posed the question, "Does the breaking of a filibuster mean bipartisanship is now alive and well or just a passing fancy?"[5] Just raising the question invites skepticism.

On July 15, 2010, the Senate passed the Dodd-Frank financial services reform bill with all Democrats and three Republicans voting for passage, but in a Google search for article titles on the subject of the bill that included the word "bipartisan," none appeared in the first 100 entries. So it appears that three is not enough, but nine seems to make the grade.

Among journalists, there is a certain amount of "cherry-picking" when it comes to identifying examples of bipartisanship. Sometimes it even helps to redefine bipartisanship to make your point. Take Katrina vanden Heuvel, editor of the left-wing periodical the *Nation,* who cited examples of bipartisan actions of which she approves, such as Democrats and Republicans collaborating on a bill to protect medical marijuana users, a bill to increase the federal minimum wage, and efforts to rein in the National Security Administration. "This collaboration," she argues, "is happening across a number of issues, but it's not bipartisanship; it's *transpartisanship*. Unlike bipartisanship, which often takes two existing view points and effectively splits the difference, transpartisanship encourages solutions that can align with many viewpoints."[6] Ms. vanden Heuvel's "transpartisanship" sounds remarkably similar to the sentiment of Senator Rand Paul (R-KY), a conservative libertarian who said in an interview that bipartisanship "is not splitting the difference. It's finding areas of common interest."[7]

There have been many examples in previous chapters of the interests of two ideologically opposite senators finding an area of overlap on which they agree, as if they are constructing a Venn diagram. Often, however, the zone of congruence is on a relatively minor topic or, at least, not a big-ticket item. The agreement between liberal Barbara Boxer and conservative James Inhofe on the importance of highways, which was described in Chapter 2, is notable, but on an issue of far greater importance—climate change—there is no agreement at all between the two.

It does stretch the imagination to accept that a vote in which virtually the entire House Democratic caucus voted against the Obamacare repeal measure was bipartisan, but the craving for the bragging rights to the bipartisan tag can sometimes seem a bit desperate. It might be surmised that the reason for this is that members of Congress believe that their constituents prefer bipartisanship to noncooperation across party lines. "Judging from recent polling, at first glance, it appears that partisan acrimony in Congress is at odds with Americans' stated desires; national poll after national poll asserts that Americans want political leaders to work together and to engage in bipartisan compromise."[8]

The operative phrase in the previous sentence is "at first glance." At second glance, one group of political scientists conducted an experiment that led them to offer another explanation: "Although people profess support for bipartisanship in an abstract sense, what they desire procedurally out of their party representatives in Congress is to *not* compromise [emphasis added] with the other side."[9]

Moreover, these same experiments came to the conclusion that the respondents "perceive outcomes closer to their own party's position as more bipartisan than compromises that provide a win for the opposing side, and observing a win by one's own party skews subsequent perceptions of bipartisan outcomes and even preferred policies."[10]

It appears that bipartisanship as a slogan is broadly favored; but when attached to a specific piece of legislation, the approval declines or, at least, comes to be defined by the partisan preferences of the respondents. Findings such as these feed skepticism about bipartisanship and augment the ranks of those who argue that it is really not such a good thing. It also points to the value of the term "bipartisan" as a slogan that proclaims the individual to whom the adjective is applied is a reasonable and responsible politician.

The Bipartisanship Deniers

Speaking ill of bipartisanship, then, might seem to be a singular act of misanthropy. If bipartisanship is the key to compromise and compromise is essential for a political system to mediate differences of opinion, only the most benighted devotees of unyielding conflict would scorn it. Surprisingly, perhaps, there is no shortage of "bipartisanship deniers."

Columnist Glenn Greenwald, who later became famous for his publication of classified materials leaked by intelligence analyst Edward Snowden, used the platform of a *New York Times* blog to make his case against bipartisanship. He wrote, "The long-standing Beltway cliché is that there is something inherently superior about 'bipartisanship' and 'centrism.' Those terms are such platitudes that they now lack any real meaning." He goes on to say that "over the last eight years, virtually every new law hailed as a shining example of bipartisanship has involved all Republicans joining with a substantial minority of Democrats to provide majoritarian support—i.e., it's been a mechanism for enacting Republican policies."[11] Greenwald sees bipartisanship as a fig leaf that conceals the surrender of Democrats. He sees Democratic votes in Congress legitimating legislation that is Republican and conservative in essence.

In the same blog dialogue, Richard Brookhiser, a senior editor at the conservative publication *National Review*, rode in from the other side of the ideological range to dismiss bipartisanship scornfully as "an empty fantasy" that is useful only during times of world conflict or civil war and a kind of ruse that papers over real policy differences.[12]

Ruth Marcus, a *Washington Post* columnist, is harshly critical of bipartisanship as a kind of collective act of denial by Democrats and Republicans to conceal their capitulation to the demands of powerful interest groups. Pointing to a vote in Congress early in 2014 to protect cost-of-living benefits for retired military personnel, Marcus laments, "Those who complain about the absence of bipartisanship in the nation's capital are sorely mistaken. When it comes to caving to a powerful constituency and bestowing benefits, bipartisanship is flourishing."[13] Her comments resemble those directed at the JOBS Act.

Yet another view suggests that Democrats and Republicans are in cahoots with one another:

> Both parties [are] getting their partisans' goodies and paying no price.... Democrats get tax breaks for green energy and unemployment extensions. Republicans get upper-bracket tax cuts and curbs in the rise of the estate tax. Though both agree on middle-class tax cuts, the deal is a dog's breakfast and the American taxpayer gets ... a

$900 billion bill.... This latest bipartisanship ... is a different and worse kind.[14]

One critic concludes with a three-part question:

So the next time you Americans hear that "partisan" is bad and "bipartisan" is good, ask yourself of bipartisanship:

1. Is it sham bipartisanship, meaning All Democrats Plus (Republican Senator) Olympia Snowe or all Republicans Plus (Democratic Senator) Ben Nelson?
2. Is it a bipartisanship that truly reflects the moderation of the American people?
3. Or is it the worst elements of both parties getting together to give each other favours and sending the bill to 2025 Generation, Screwed Over Lane, Debtsville, DC?

If the answer is (3), ask yourself if you wouldn't mind a bit more partisanship.[15]

With the retirement of Senator Snowe in 2013, her replacement as the senator willing to apply the coloration of bipartisanship has been Senator Susan Collins, also a Maine Republican. On April 2, 2014, Collins announced, along with her Maine colleague, independent Angus King, that they would support Intelligence Committee chair Dianne Feinstein's motion to declassify a report on the CIA's secret interrogation program.

By itself, Collins's support for declassification of the report would have given Feinstein the bare majority of the fifteen-member committee that she needed to declassify the report and send it to President Obama, who could make it public. As the sole defector from the committee Republicans, Collins's vote would certainly have been an example of "sham bipartisanship," but Collins triggered a broader Republican defection that included

Richard Burr of North Carolina and the ranking Republican, Saxby Chambliss of Georgia, that ultimately resulted in an 11–3 vote to declassify. One Republican senator voted "present."[16]

Collins's actions point out a flaw in the arguments of the bipartisanship deniers. By announcing her support for declassification, she gave Chairwoman Feinstein the majority she needed to get the document released. That had the effect of inducing the two Republicans who had previously been on the fence over the issue to support the disclosures. In a Senate in which the numbers of Democrats and Republicans are so close, a single defection on one side that makes a majority may induce others to get on the winning side. It may be then that the single vote from the other side does more than just provide a veneer of bipartisanship. Nonetheless, scathing attacks on bipartisanship ring in from all sides.

Correspondent Kevin D. Williamson, writing in the *National Review Online,* charges that "for more than a decade now, the operating model in Congress has been that Democrats more or less support Republicans' tax cuts (though sometimes howling about it for the benefit of their base), while in return Republicans support Democrats' spending (also howling about it). That is the substance of the national suicide pact that Congress has signed us up for."[17]

Writing at the time that the nation was in the depths of the Great Recession, columnist Thomas Frank, a liberal, attacked the tendency of bipartisanship advocacy to be burdened with nostalgia: "It's supposed to be high-minded stuff, this longing for a golden age. But in some ways it is the most cynical stance possible. It takes no idea seriously, since everything is up for compromise. The role of political parties is merely to cancel each other out, so that only the glorious centrists remain, triangulating majestically between obnoxious extremes." On a despairing note, Frank concludes, "Never has Beltway orthodoxy looked as clueless and futile as it does today. Confronted with the greatest economic failure in decades, it demands that the president make common cause with people for whom those failed ideas are still sacred."[18]

Good versus Bad Bipartisanship

Those who criticize bipartisanship often present specific pieces of legislation they find especially odious that were enacted with two-party support. Matt Purple, writing in the conservative journal the *American Spectator*, points to two examples of bad bipartisanship: the 1986 immigration reform bill known as Simpson-Mazzoli for its authors, which "passed a Democratic House and Republican senate and was signed into law by President Ronald Reagan, [and] twenty years later, Simpson-Mazzoli was regarded as a failure that had granted amnesty to illegal immigrants while doing nothing to control the border."[19]

His second statutory scourge is the "No Child Left Behind" law that he characterizes as "one of the great policy flops of our time." He quotes the *Washington Post*'s conclusion that "a review of a decade of evidence demonstrates the NCLB has failed both in terms of its own policy goals and more broadly." The quest for bipartisanship, he concludes, is "all based on the flawed premise that bipartisan is better. Imagine a line with two poles at the end, one labeled 'liberal' and the other labeled 'conservative.' Simply because a law occupies a median point on the line doesn't mean that it's somehow more virtuous—or even remotely effective."[20]

It seems as if all commentators can find a piece of legislation that they hate and blame its deficiencies on bipartisanship. The critics of President Obama's Affordable Care Act may find it defective in many ways, but bipartisanship was not one of its defects. The legislation passed only with Democratic votes.

But what in particular about bipartisanship seems so problematic in the eyes of its critics? In the comments of Katrina vanden Heuvel on the left and Senator Rand Paul on the right, the problem is that lawmaking involves "splitting the difference" rather than finding convergent areas of agreement.

What constitutes "good" or bad" bipartisanship is obviously subjective. Bipartisanship involves more than the joint sponsorship of legislation. There can also be bipartisanship to block legislation. One example comes from the Senate committee known for its bipartisanship, the Agriculture Committee, where a coalition of four Democrats and eight Republicans blocked a proposal from their committee colleague, Senator Tom Harkin (D-IA), to have the federal government keep tabs on the snacks sold in school vending machines. Harkin's concern was that "junk food" was common in the vending machines and he wanted the federal government to set guidelines for the schools and provide incentives for making healthier snacks available. The defeat of Harkin's amendment caused the nonpartisan Center for Science in the Public Interest to send out a press release sardonically titled "Junk Food in Schools Enjoys Bipartisan Support."[21]

Opponents of Harkin's amendment argued that school food policy should be a matter of local control and should not involve the federal government. On the face of it, this argument is a very common one made by those who consider the federal government too intrusive, but supporters of Harkin's amendment pointed out that opponents used local control as a fig leaf to cover the nakedness of their desire to stuff school children with fattening junk food. As one Harkin supporter charged, "We know that soda and junk food marketers do not really support 'local control,' because they fight like heck when we try to get junk food out of the schools at the local level."[22]

Transactional Bipartisanship versus Values Bipartisanship

Transactional bipartisanship develops more readily in Congress because it involves dollars and cents and lends itself to "splitting the difference." The budget agreement worked out by Senator Patty Murray and Representative Paul Ryan at the end of 2013 was a good example of transactional bipartisanship. Involving as it does budget and appropriations, it is important legislation; and because of the magnitude involved and the fact that it is a classic example of "split the difference" bipartisanship, it presents a very inviting target for critics of bipartisanship.

So long as dollars and cents are involved, a path to bipartisanship becomes easier, but when legislation, which usually comes down to a duel over numbers, is transformed into a struggle over values, the likelihood of bipartisan agreement diminishes. But numbers can be tantamount to values when large amounts are added or deleted from major pieces of legislation.

Such was the case with the farm bill that Congress is required to reauthorize every five years. This bill began its legislative journey in the Senate on May 14, 2013, when the Agriculture Committee passed its farm bill. As we discussed in Chapter 2, the Senate Agriculture Committee has a record of being one of the least ideologically polarized committees in the Senate, and less than a month later the Senate passed the committee's bill by unanimous consent. The House Agriculture Committee also passed a farm bill a day after the Senate Agriculture Committee passed its bill, but when the bill got to the House floor a month later, it failed to pass.[23]

At this point, the process went off the rails, and in July the House stripped out the portion of the bill that authorizes SNAP (Supplemental Nutrition Assistance Program), better known as "food stamps." The combining of farm legislation with food stamps dates back to the 1977 farm bill and was designed to generate support among agricultural interests for programs that feed the poor and, reciprocally, to persuade urban and minority members to cast their votes for legislation that benefitted farmers and agribusiness. This commonality of interests was severed when House Majority Leader Eric Cantor supported a farm bill that had nothing for SNAP.[24]

Cantor and the Republican leadership were being cross-pressured by members of their caucus affiliated with the Tea Party, except those who represented rural districts. The farm-state members wanted a farm bill—with or without food stamps—and the Tea Party affiliates argued that the nutrition program was plagued with fraud and fostered dependency on the federal government.

Stripped of its transactional cladding of dollars to farmers and food stamps to the poor, the bill became a struggle over values, and bipartisanship succumbed to ideological polarization. Eventually a conference committee reconciled the differences between the House and Senate bills, and the legislation was signed by President Obama in February 2014.

In the end, the farm bill did "split the difference," but the threat of eliminating the food stamp program from a farm bill where it had been comfortably ensconced since 1977 endangered the legislation by shifting it away from a battle over dollars and cents and directly into the zone of maximum partisan antagonism. In that zone there could be no bipartisan convergence because it did not include only provisions on which both parties could agree.

Transactional bipartisanship, which seems to trouble some people because "it becomes a code word for 'we're willing to compromise everything just to get one more person from the other side on board,"[25] becomes—in the words of Christopher Hitchens—"the false security of consensus."[26]

The Bipartisanship of Small Achievements

The peril in defining bipartisanship strictly in terms of legislation on which most members of both parties agree leads to a bipartisanship of small achievements. When we learned on March 5, 2014, that "a powerful bipartisan group of senators are introducing a resolution on Wednesday afternoon condemning Russia's intervention into Ukraine,"[27] were we heartened that somehow this demonstrates the vitality of bipartisanship?

The first week of March 2014 saw the Senate approve two bipartisan bills. The first was a bill to reduce the premiums homeowners pay for flood insurance and the second reauthorized a federally subsidized child-care program. Both bills passed with sizeable bipartisan majorities: the flood insurance bill passed 72–22 and the child-care bill by an even more impressive 96–2. About the same time, a bill to extend unemployment benefits to the long-term unemployed was put together by a bipartisan group of ten senators and sent to the floor of the Senate. The bipartisan pedigree of the two bills that passed the Senate was impeccable by any standard. A harder question to answer is, did they mean anything?

The desire of lawmakers to earn the bipartisan seal of approval may cause them to boast a bit too energetically about a bill than its importance warrants. Was the child-care reauthorization bill important enough to give a major infusion of life into the sickly body of bipartisanship? Probably not. After all, it was only the reauthorization of legislation already on the books, and the purpose of the new bill was merely to update federal standards for child care.[28]

Like the child-care bill, the flood insurance bill modified a previous piece of legislation, in this case the Biggert-Waters National Flood Insurance Act of 2012, a law just two years old. The pattern of voting on the bill is quite revealing. All Senate Democrats except two supported the bill, as did every Republican from a state with a coastline except Richard Shelby of Alabama and John Cornyn of Texas. Georgia Republican Johnny Isakson, however, was rapturous in his praise: "I am thrilled the Senate was able to come together in a bipartisan manner today to protect millions of hardworking families across the country from the steep increases in their annual flood insurance premiums."[29] According to the Insurance

Information Institute, 18 percent of Americans have flood insurance. This number presumably refers to homeowners rather than the total population, but nevertheless, it is not an insignificant number of people who are affected. It does not, however, affect most Americans. It is a statute of modest importance but perhaps not worthy of the effusive words of its co-sponsor, New Jersey Democrat Robert Menendez: "Thanks to a strong bipartisan effort, we have averted [a] manmade perfect storm."[30]

The uplifting words of these senators mask the underlying flaw in the bill, which is that it can be seen as an incentive to moral hazard by encouraging the rebuilding of homes in areas that might well be subject to future flooding and the need for additional money for rebuilding. It becomes the kind of legislation that bipartisanship deniers rightly deride. As for the bill that would have provided unemployment benefits for several million Americans who had exhausted their benefits, it became another piece of message legislation with little hope of passage.

Good Things in Small Packages?

It would be easy to dismiss bills of modest scope that skirt the ideological fault lines as what is known derisively in Washington as "small ball" and bipartisan "tokenism." And it is true that they are not major tax reforms or national infrastructure bills or legislation to put the nation's costly entitlement programs on a sustainable basis, but if those bills of broad scope are beyond the reach of the present Congress, are the bills that the Senate manages to pass just so many empty boxes, or could they be those good things that come in small packages?

Individually, the bills may be of only moderate importance, but that raises the question of whether, in the aggregate, a collection of modest bipartisan bills passed at a time of partisan gridlock qualify as a vital sign of bipartisanship in the Senate?

As we have seen in the case of the hastily enacted STOCK Act, the desire for a showing of bipartisanship can produce results of dubious quality. We would certainly not assign much importance to "commemorative" bills honoring various civic groups or bills naming federal buildings that pass with whopping bipartisan majorities as major achievements, but there is another way to look at the Senate's less-than-sensational acts of bipartisanship.

Just before the Senate passed the child-care bill, Ed O'Keefe and Paul Kane, who cover Congress for the *Washington Post*, characterized the bill as "a small, noncontroversial program that is likely to pass," but quickly added, "In this case, it's not the 'what' of the effort that's most important, but the 'how.'"[31] They then sketched the background of how the child-care reauthorization came to be in a polarized Senate by focusing on two senators, Charles Schumer (D-NY) and Lamar Alexander (R-TN), who orchestrated a plan to allow legislation to be debated and amended. They did this by collaborating to circumvent the procedural dueling between the majority leader and the Republicans. These were the clashes in which Reid blocked Republican amendments that he thought were designed to embarrass Democrats and the Republicans retaliated with filibusters.

Schumer and Alexander are not natural allies. Apart from their partisan and regional differences, since 2010 Schumer has been the Democrat responsible for framing the party's message in his capacity as chairman of the Democratic Policy Committee. This places him in charge of the "war room," the Democratic Policy and Communications Center. His public statements have tended to be partisan and provocative, as would be expected from the person responsible for messaging. Until 2011, Alexander had been Schumer's counterpart and had been responsible for presenting the GOP side in the most forceful terms.

Despite these responsibilities, which would seem to make them the unlikeliest of partners, one factor, often overlooked in explaining the disposition of senators to work together, may play a role in promoting cooperation between them: both are long-serving members of the Senate and both served as members of the Rules Committee at the same time. "I've been here fourteen years and Alexander has been here about eleven," Schumer said. "But we were there, both of us were there and remember when the Senate used to legislate, and thoroughly enjoyed it and wish it would return."[32]

The modern Senate bears little resemblance to the Senate of a half-century ago, when senators spent less time raising money for campaigns and decamping from Washington on Thursday afternoons, not to return until late Monday so as to been seen by constituents in their states over the weekend.

Since the extramural lives of senators no longer revolve around their colleagues, what goes on within the chamber itself remains the only setting for sustained contact. As we have seen, due to their compactness, the committees promote interaction among senators. The multiple committee assignments of senators, as opposed to the more limited committee responsibilities of House members and the larger membership of House committees, creates certain conditions in the Senate that promote bipartisan contact, if not bipartisanship.

As Senator John Boozman, the Arkansas Republican, explained it,

> The thing about the Senate is that we are a very small group and in the House, if you were on the Appropriations Committee, you would only be on the Appropriations Committee. And you'd probably have three subcommittees on Appropriations and nothing else. In the Senate, we have the same number of committees and (Appropriations) subcommittees as the House does, only we have a lot fewer people on the Senate side. I've got five subcommittees on Appropriations and I'm also on Agriculture and Veterans' Affairs and I am ranking on subcommittees on both Environment and Public Works and Ag.

The reason I say this is that somebody I serve on Appropriations with—and I use Bernie Sanders (I-VT) as an example—I also serve on Veterans Affairs and EPW with him. So you have a lot of interactions with these people in various different areas and you get to know them pretty well.[33]

Sanders would seem an unlikely legislative partner for a Republican. He is a self-proclaimed Socialist and a supporter of the "Occupy Wall Street" movement, yet his cooperation with Republicans is by no means rare.

In 2014, when a scandal erupted over the quality of care in hospitals run by the Department of Veterans Affairs, he teamed with Senator John McCain on a bill to hire more doctors and nurses and to authorize the secretary of veterans affairs to more easily fire incompetent administrators. Of the bill, McCain said, "Can we sort of pledge that we are committed to seeing this all the way through? I would urge our colleagues to do that. Let's not get hung up on certain aspects of our differences that most people would view as gridlock in this body."[34] McCain's advice evokes the search for areas of common agreement that characterize so much of the bipartisanship in the Senate and that I heard so often in my interviews.

Examples such as this of bipartisan cooperation would, of course, be multiplied for those senators who have been in the Senate the longest. This, however, is not to suggest that newcomers to the Senate are less likely to be bipartisan. Senator Mark Warner of Virginia made the cultivation of bipartisanship an important cause as a first-term member, and other newcomers have quickly sensed that bipartisan relationships can be useful.

Warner's seventy-six meetings, dinners, retreats, and conference calls with colleagues encompassed a wide and divergent group of senators that included twenty-six Democrats and twenty-one Republicans. A number of the latter were Republicans who came to the Senate in the so-called "Tea Party" election of 2010. Others were part of the group that Sean Theriault dubbed "Gingrich" senators, former Republican members of the House elected in the mid 1990s.[35] While the roll-call voting records of Warner's Republican invitees show little convergence with those of Democrats, the differences were not so great as to preclude attendance. At a time at which the mere association with Democrats can spell trouble for a Republican with members of the party base, such a willingness to come together is a small but significant indicator of the existence of Senate bipartisanship.

Unicameral Bipartisanship: The Sound of One Hand Clapping

Half of the twelve senators I interviewed had previously served as members of the House of Representatives and were able to supply a bicameral perspective. One of them, Mike Crapo (R-ID), retained warm thoughts about his time in the House but saw distinct differences with regard to bipartisanship in the two chambers:

> In the House, 218 votes, a majority, is 100% of the power, and that power is exercised with an iron fist by the majority. Bipartisanship happens in the House when the majority decides that it's a positive thing to do. In the Senate, it happens when you can't move the legislation.[36]

We have seen that bipartisanship in the Senate is not a rarity in its standing committees, and we have even seen instances of legislation getting to the floor and passing the Senate with impressively large bipartisan majorities. But such legislation, if it is to be signed into law, must pass a House of Representatives that is, by its very nature, not disposed to bipartisanship. Added to that fact are certain partisan principles such as the "Hastert rule," which is less a rule than a tactic that requires virtual unanimity among House Republicans before a bill will be brought to the floor. While there is no comparable "Reid rule" in the Senate, the majority leader would be unlikely to bring up legislation opposed by substantial numbers of his caucus.

In the highly partisan atmosphere of the contemporary Congress, party leaders in both houses will not even consider bringing up bills that track too closely to bills passed by the other chamber for fear of being drawn into a House-Senate conference in which distasteful subject matter will be on the table. The comprehensive immigration bill passed by the Senate was considered unacceptable to most House Republicans, so no immigration legislation of any kind was considered, thus avoiding the trap of being caught in a conference. Likewise, House legislation approving the Keystone XL pipeline from the tar sands of Alberta, Canada, to the US Gulf Coast has caused Senate Democrats to shun energy legislation because they fear the pipeline as a Republican bargaining chip.

Cyclical Bipartisanship

In this book I have evaluated the vitality of bipartisanship largely in spatial terms (committee versus floor action), in terms of scope (breadth or narrowness of legislation), and in terms of substance (values versus numbers). There is also a temporal dimension based upon the political calendar and where in the electoral cycle a bill's author might be.

You may recall the description in Chapter 4 of how Majority Leader Reid opposed a bipartisan amendment sponsored by Democrat Kirsten Gillibrand and Republican Scott Brown because Brown, who had been elected to serve out the term of Democrat Edward M. Kennedy, was up for reelection.

Cooperation across the partisan aisle is often influenced by whether the sponsor of a bill is "in cycle" or not. As Reid would not want to give politically useful cover to Brown, Republicans in 2014 were not eager to help out Democrats up for reelection in November of that year.

But there is another side to these kinds of calculations: if a bill is truly popular or noncontroversial, opposing it simply to deny the opposition an electoral advantage can backfire. Alaska Republican Lisa Murkowski reflected on this dilemma:

> I'm probably not a good politician, because this business about not giving somebody an issue in a campaign if it's an important policy issue that needs to be resolved, can't we just advance it for the right reasons? People will read that quote and say, "Well, there's Pollyanna again." And you can tell I'm not in cycle, so it makes it easier to say. But I would say it even if I were in cycle.[37]

In answering the question posed in the title of this book, it occurred to me that I should not have posed it in such stark terms. In the Senate, at least, bipartisanship can never be totally dead because to achieve anything at all, even in the chamber's present partisan configuration, bipartisan sponsorship is virtually mandatory. With only a handful of seats separating Democrats and Republicans, a bill with only Democratic or Republican names would stand little chance of passage. On the other hand, from the perspective of party leaders, such coauthorship could be the kiss of death, especially when a cosponsor from the opposition is up for reelection. We have also seen that the seeds of bipartisanship sown in committee can perish in the more contentious terrain of the Senate floor. Within a single twenty-four-hour period in 2014, there was both dramatic evidence of the vitality of bipartisanship and an event that augurs ill for it.

Such a day was the evening of Tuesday, June 13, 2014, when Washington, DC, learned the shocking news that Representative Eric Cantor, the majority leader of the House, the chamber's second-ranking Republican, had been defeated for renomination in Virginia's seventh congressional district. The defeat of a party leader in a primary is an unprecedented event. Much of the interpretation of why Cantor lost to an obscure economics professor was that he was seen as too willing to consider immigration reform.[38] Cantor's defeat sealed the fate of immigration reform in the Republican-controlled House. There would be no chance of any negotiation of the Senate's comprehensive immigration reform bill.

On the very next day, on the other side of Capitol Hill, the Senate, by a 93–3 bipartisan vote, passed the Sanders-McCain bill to reform the medical services of the Department of Veterans Affairs. The House had passed a bill that was similar, but not identical, to the Senate bill. The chairman of the Senate Veterans' Affairs Committee, Senator Sanders, said, "The [House and Senate] bills have a lot in common. There are some differences, but I think that [House Veterans' Affairs Committee Chairman] Jeff Miller is a reasonable guy, and I think we are going to work them out."[39]

So the answer to the question, "Is bipartisanship dead?" needs to be qualified. It is not dead, but it has its good days and its bad days.

Stepping Back

One can become so tightly focused on the mechanics of bipartisanship or its absence that its larger implications become lost. Accordingly, a few parting thoughts about bipartisanship in the Senate are in order:

A consistently liberal or conservative voting record on the part of senators is no obstacle to bipartisan cooperation. Indeed, such a clear-cut ideological voting pattern may serve as useful political cover for important bipartisan action if a senator is disposed to use it. Such was the case with Pennsylvania

Republican Pat Toomey's partnership with West Virginia Democrat Joe Manchin on a bill to strengthen background checks for firearms purchases in the aftermath of the mass killings at Sandy Hook Elementary School in Newtown, Connecticut.

While it is certainly true that it was in the political interest of Senator Toomey, who represents a state won by President Obama in 2012, to ingratiate himself with moderate voters, there was a risk involved that antagonizing gun-rights advocates might, in the future, lead to a primary election challenge.

A distinction needs to be made between bipartisan voting behavior and bipartisan relationships among senators. This has important implications for the Senate as an institution. Connections across party lines that arise in the relative intimacy of a committee or in the Senate gym enable conversations to take place that can prime senators for future bipartisan cooperation, even if there are no immediate payoffs. "Friendliness," in itself, may yield valuable, albeit unpredictable, dividends.

The extreme polarization of Senate politics does not mean that the institution is so incapacitated that it cannot respond to emergencies. The scandal that enveloped the Department of Veterans Affairs in 2014 involved fraudulent scheduling practices that delayed needed treatment for ex-service members in hospitals run by the department. The Senate acted with speed—some might even say alacrity—with the Sanders-McCain bill, which saw the partnership of two of the most ideologically disparate senators in fashioning legislation to deal with the problem.

But a cautionary note is needed here. In their haste to come up with a fix for the problem, lawmakers overlooked one significant feature of their handiwork: its price-tag of $50 billion annually, a staggering amount that could gut other parts of the federal government.

As we saw in the case of the ill-fated STOCK Act, bipartisan means do not always produce sensible ends. Indeed, there may be a case to be made—and critics of bipartisanship would be inclined to make it—that cobbling together a bipartisan coalition is more likely to produce bad legislation because of the very many trade-offs the bill may require.

Most important of all, of course, is that there are limits set on the capacity of the Senate to be bipartisan by the American electorate. Sailing against the wind is not something that the elected representatives of the American people can accomplish on a consistent basis. And would we want them to? Defying public opinion in pursuit of an inner Burkean ideal is not something that voters would tolerate for very long. This does not imply, of course, that the Senate must always be precisely aligned with the philosophical divisions in the electorate, but it is simply a recognition of the fact that there are issues on which no consensus can be achieved.

The inability to find agreement on a matter with which, one might think, no reasonable person would find fault is no failure of politics. It is politics. And it involves the hard, exhausting work of persuasion. It is achieved by recruiting the right candidates, raising the considerable amounts of money that modern campaigns require, and giving the voters real alternatives. That this may result in more polarization—the very negation of bipartisanship—is one of the risks we run in a representative republic that offers none of the comfortable certainties of authoritarian rule.

Notes

Introduction

1. See: Keith T. Poole and Howard Rosenthal, *Congress, A Political-Economic History of Roll Call Voting* (New York: Oxford University Press, 1997).

2. The term was popularized by Sidney Blumenthal in his book *The Permanent Campaign* (Boston: Beacon Press, 1980), in which Blumenthal characterizes it as "the 'game plan' for the embattled politician. He is increasingly beleaguered because he fails to distinguish between governing and campaigning" (p. 8).

3. Frances E. Lee, "Making Laws and Making Points: Senate Governance in an Era of Uncertain Majorities," *The Forum* 9, no. 4, 15.

Chapter 1

1. Michael Kranish, Brian C. Mooney, and Nina J. Easton, *John F. Kerry* (New York: Public Affairs, 2004), 268.

2. Author's telephone interview with Paul Kane, Washington, DC, Dec. 7, 2012.

3. Ibid.

4. The following month, Alexander figured prominently at the second inauguration of President Obama by delivering a brief statement despite the possibility that some of his anti-Obama constituents might object to his presence on the stand.

5. Author's telephone interview with Senator Johnny Isakson, Dec. 13, 2012.

6. "Lame Duck Session Not the Time for New Treaty Ratifications," *Mike Lee Blog* (Sept. 24, 2012) http://www.lee.senate.gov/public /index.cfm/2012/9/lame-duck-session-not-the-time-for-new-treaty -ratifications. Accessed July 8, 2014.

7. Ibid.

8. Ibid.

9. Tom Strode, "Sen. Defeats Treaty Opposed by Family Groups," *Baptist Press* (Dec. 4, 2012) http://www.bpnews.net /printerfriendly.asp?id=39290. Accessed July 8, 2014.

10. "Senator Kerry: Objections to Disabilities Treaty Don't Stand Up to Scrutiny," United States Senate Committee on Foreign Relations press release (Dec. 4, 2012) http://www.foreign.senate.gov/press/chair /release/senator-kerry-objections-to-disabilities-treaty-dont-stand-up-to -scutiny. Accessed July 29, 2014.

11. US Congress, Senate, 112th Congress, 2nd session, July 31, 2012, Committee on Foreign Relations, Treaty Doc. 112-7, "Convention on the Rights of Persons with Disabilities," passim.

12. Remarks by Senator John McCain at the 2012 Human Rights Summit, Dec. 5, 2012, Washington, D.C. http://www.mccain.senate .gov/public/index.cfm/speeches?ID=6bf4624f-db22-1948-eeed -478d3a8c78a0. Accessed July 29, 2014.

13. See: Harold W. Stanley and Richard G. Niemi, *Vital Statistics on American Politics, 2011–2012* (Los Angeles: CQ/Sage Press, 2011), 205–206.

Chapter 2

1. Richard F. Fenno, Jr., *Congressmen in Committees* (Boston: Little, Brown, 1973).

2. Ibid.

3. C. Lawrence Evans, "Congressional Committees," in *The Oxford Handbook of the American Congress*, eds. Eric Schickler and Frances E. Lee (New York: Oxford University Press, 2011), 398.

4. Fenno, *Congressmen in Committees*, 59.

5. Author's telephone interview with Foreign Relations Committee staff member, Dec. 10, 2012.

6. Ibid.

7. Burgess Everett, "Robert Menendez: GOP 'Highly Partisan' on Ukraine," *Politico* (May 6, 2014) http://www.politico.com/story /2014/05/senate-foreign-relations-divided-on-ukraine-106395.html. Accessed July 8, 2014.

8. See: Jeremy W. Peters, "Bitterly Divided Senate Panel Backs Hagel for Defense," *New York Times* (Feb. 12, 2013); Michael A, Memoli, "Hagel's Defense Nomination OKd by Senate Committee," *Los Angeles Times* (Feb. 12, 2013) http://articles.latimes.com/2013 /feb/12/nation/la-na-hagel-nomination-20130213; and Alexis Levinson, "Senate Armed Services Committee Approves Hagel Nomination," *The Daily Caller* (Feb. 12, 2013) http://dailycaller.com/2013/02/12 /senate-armed-services-committee-approves-hagel-nomination/. Both accessed July 8, 2014.

9. Author's telephone interview with Senator Mark Begich, Dec. 18, 2012.

10. Author's telephone interview with staff member of the Senate Committee on Armed Services, Feb. 21, 2013.

11. Ibid.

12. Michael Barone and Chuck McCutcheon, eds., *The Almanac of American Politics, 2012* (Chicago; University of Chicago Press, 2011), 491.

13. Traditionally, senators were inclined to favor nominees from their own ranks and dispensed with hearings altogether. This changed in 1937, when a motion to take up the nomination of Senator Hugo Black (D-MS), a sitting senator, was objected to by two colleagues. Ultimately, he was endorsed by a 5–1 vote of the Judiciary Committee. (See Roger K. Newman, *Hugo Black, A Biography* [New York: Pantheon, 1994], 238.) Less fortunate was Senator John Tower (R-TX), a former chairman of the Armed Services Committee nominated to be secretary of defense in 1989. Despite a favorable vote in the Armed Services Committee, Tower was rejected 47–53 in a confirmation vote.

14. Karen Parrish, "Panetta Lauds Nominees for Defense Secretary, CIA Director," US Department of Defense (Jan. 7, 2013) http://www .defense.gov/news/newsarticle.aspx?id=118929. Accessed July 29, 2014.

15. Elizabeth Drew, *Citizen McCain* (New York: Simon & Schuster, 2002), 18.

16. Drew, *Citizen McCain*, 25.

17. Rowan Scarborough, "Hagel's Foreign Policy Record Could Doom His Chances for Top Pentagon Post," *Washington Times* (Dec. 30, 2012).

18. US Congress, Senate, 113th Congress, 1st sess., Committee on Armed Services, "Business Meeting to Consider the Nomination of Charles T. Hagel to Be Secretary of Defense," (Feb. 12, 2013), 13.

19. Ibid. 19–21.

20. Ibid.

21. Ibid., 24.

22. Ibid., 26.

23. Ibid.

24. Jennifer Steinhauer, "Complex Fight in Senate Over Curbing Military Sex Assaults," *New York Times* (June 14, 2013) http://www.nytimes.com/2013/06/15/us/politics/in-senate-complex-fight-over-curbing-sexual-military-assaults.html?pagewanted=all. Accessed July 8, 2014.

25. Author's telephone interview with Senator Debbie Stabenow, March 26, 2013.

26. Ibid.

27. Ibid.

28. Author's telephone interview with Agriculture Committee staff member, March 8, 2013.

29. Author's telephone interview with Senator Patrick Leahy, March 14, 2013.

30. Richard F. Fenno, Jr., *Congressmen in Committees* (Boston: Little, Brown, 1973), 2.

31. "Inhofe Ranked Most Conservative Senator, Sherrod Brown Most Liberal," cnsnews.com (March 1, 2010) http://cnsnews.com/news/article/inhofe-ranked-most-conservative-senator-sherrod-brown-most-liberal. Accessed July 29, 2014.

32. Author's telephone interview with Senator Barbara Boxer, Dec. 21, 2012.

33. Burgess Everett and Adam Snider, "Barbara Boxer-David Vitter Feud Draws Blood," *Politico* (Sept. 16, 2013) http://www.politico.com/story/2013/09/barbara-boxer-david-vitter-obamacare-feud-96888.html. Accessed July 28, 2014.

34. Ibid.

35. Ibid.

36. Author's telephone interview, May 12, 2012.

37. Sean M. Theriault, *The Gingrich Senators* (New York: Oxford University Press, 2013) p. 174.

38. Ibid.

Chapter 3

1. Author's telephone interviews with Senator Mark Begich, Dec. 18, 2012, and Senator Debbie Stabenow, March 26, 2013.

2. Author's telephone interview with Senator Mark Warner, June 3, 2013.

3. Author's telephone interview with Senator John Boozman, May 9, 2013.

4. Author's telephone interview with Senator Mike Johanns, Dec. 19, 2012.

5. Author's telephone interview with Senator Mike Crapo, Dec. 21, 2012.

6. Karoun Demirjian, "Reid Juggles Eight-State Strategy to Protect Democratic Majority," *Las Vegas Sun* (July 26, 2012) http://www .lasvegassun.com/news/2012/jul/26/reid-juggles-eight-state-strategy -protect-democrat/. Accessed July 29, 2014.

7. US Congress (Senate) 113th Congress, 2nd. sess, *Congressional Record,* April 30, 2014, p. S2536.

8. Author's telephone interview with Senator Mark Warner, June 3, 2013.

9. Frances E. Lee, "Making Laws and Making Points: Senate Governance in an Era of Uncertain Majorities," *The Forum* 9, no. 4 (2011), 15.

10. Reid Cherlin, "We Do Anything They Ask: How the NRA's Grading System Keeps Congress in Lockdown," *GQ* (July 24, 2012) http://www.gq.com/news-politics/blogs/death-race/2012/07/nra -grades-and-congress.html. Accessed July 8, 2014.

11. Linda Greenhouse, "The N.R.A. at the Bench," *Opinionator* (Dec. 26, 2012) http://opinionator.blogs.nytimes.com/2012/12/26 /the-n-r-a-at-the-bench/?_php=true&_type=blogs&_r=0. Accessed July 8, 2014.

12. Jim Geraghty, "The NRA Will Be Scoring the Background-Check," *National Review Online* (April 11, 2013) http://www .nationalreview.com/campaign-spot/345310/nra-will-be-scoring -background-check-vote. Accessed July 8, 2014.

13. Gerald F. Seib, "Manchin Describes the Effect of an NRA 'Score'," *Wall Street Journal* (April 18, 2013) http://blogs.wsj.com /washwire/2013/04/18manchin-describes-the-effect. Accessed July 8, 2014.

14. Sari Horowitz, "Senate Confirms ATF Director," *Washington Post* (July 31, 2013) http://www.washingtonpost.com/world/national -security/senate-confirms-atf-director/2013/07/31/dc9b0644-fa09 -11e2-8752-b41d7ed1f685_story.html. Accessed July 29, 2014.

15. Barbara Sinclair, *Party Wars* (Norman, OK: University of Oklahoma Press, 2006), 211.

16. Richard A. Arenberg and Robert B. Dove, *Defending The Filibuster* (Bloomington, IN: Indiana University Press, 2012), 48.

17. Bill Dauster, "It's Not *Mr. Smith Goes to Washington*," *Washington Monthly* (Nov. 1996), 34.

18. Glenn Kessler, "Four Pinocchios for Obama's Claim That Republicans Have 'Filibustered about 500 Pieces of Legislation," *Washington Post* (May 9, 2014). http://www.washingtonpost.com/blogs /fact-checker/wp/2014/05/09/four-pinocchios-for-obamas-claim -that-republicans-have-filibustered-about-500-pieces-of-legislation/. Accessed July 29, 2014.

19. Author's telephone interview with Senator Mike Johanns, Dec. 19, 2012.

20. David A. Farenthold, "Why the Senate Likes to 'Gang' Around," *Washington Post* (May 6, 2011) http://www.washingtonpost .com/politics/why-the-senate-likes-to-gang-around/2011/05/04 /AFvbXJCG_story.html. Accessed July 29, 2014.

21. David Hawkings, "Gangs in Congress Go Where Partisans Fear To Tread," *Roll Call* (April 25, 2013), http://blogs.rollcall.com /hawkings/gangs-in-congress. Accessed July 8, 2014.

22. Author's telephone interview with Senator Mark Warner, June 3, 2013.

23. Ibid.

24. Ross K. Baker, *Friend and Foe in the U.S. Senate* (New York: The Free Press, 1980), 45.

25. See: Jonathan Weisman, "With a Bipartisan Flurry, Becoming a Do-Something Senate," *New York Times* (May 25, 2012); Scott Wong, "Senate Tries Bipartisanship," *Politico* (April 1, 2012); and Meredith Shiner, "Senate Revives Lawmaking," *The Hill* (April 30, 2012).

26. Author's telephone interview with Senator Mike Johanns, Dec. 19, 2012.

27. Ryan Lizza, "Getting to Maybe," *New Yorker* (June 24, 2013), 47.

28. "Warner: Gang of Six May Touch Social Security," *Politico* (April 17, 2011).

29. Barbara Sinclair, *Unorthodox Lawmaking* (Washington, DC: CQ Press, 2012), 56.

30. Author's telephone interview with Senator Mike Crapo, Dec. 21, 2012.

31. Rule XV, paragraph 5, of the Standing Rules of the Senate.

Chapter 4

1. See: Hugh Heclo, "Issue Networks and the Executive Establishment," in *The New American Political System*, ed. Anthony King (Washington, DC: American Enterprise Institute, 1978), 87–124; and Gordon Adams, *The Iron Triangle: The Politics of Defense Contracting* (New York: Council on Economic Priorities, 1981).

2. See: Barry R. Weingast and William J. Marshall, "The Industrial Organization of Congress: or, Why Legislatures, Like Firms, Are Not Organized as Markets," *Journal of Political Economy* 96, no. 1 (Feb. 1988) 132–163.

3. See: Tim Groseclose, "The Committee Outlier Debate: A Review and Reexamination of Some of the Evidence," *Public Choice* 80, 265–273; and Bruce A. Ray, "The Responsiveness of the U.S. Congressional Armed Services Committees to Their Parent Bodies," *Legislative Studies Quarterly* 5, no.4 (Nov. 1980), 501–515.

4. Sheryl Gay Stolberg, "Baucus, Conflicted Architect of Health Overhaul, Is Obama's Pick for China," *New York Times* (Dec. 18, 2013) http://www.nytimes.com/2013/12/19/us/politics/baucus still -fretting-over-health-law-he-shepherded.html?pagewanted=all&_r=0. Accessed July 29, 2014.

5. Note that this "Gang of Six" is not the group of the same name that proposed budget cuts to reduce the federal deficit at the end of 2010. The Senate's propensity to give birth to "gangs" can cause people to confuse which particular gang is being referenced.

6. "Republican Senator Hears Health Care Concerns Back Home," *CNN Politics* (Aug. 18, 2009) http://www.cnn.com/2009 /POLITICS/08/12/health.care.grassley. Accessed July 8, 2014.

7. Ezra Klein, "Chuck Grassley Fundraises Against

Health-Care Reform," *Washington Post* (Aug. 31, 2009) http://voices
.washingtonpost.com/ezra-klein/2009/08/chuck_grassley_fundraises
_agai.html. Accessed July 17, 2014.

8. "What the 'Gang of Four' Wants from the Health Care Bill,"
NPR Transcripts, Sept. 9, 2009.

9. Ibid.

10. Olympia Snowe, *Fighting for Common Ground* (Philadelphia:
Weinstein Books, 2013), 196–197.

11. Carrie Budoff Brown, "Senate Finance Approves Health Bill,"
Pittsburgh Post-Gazette (Oct. 14, 2009) http://www.post-gazette.com
/news/politics-politico/2009/10/14/Senate-Finance-approves-health
-bill/stories/200910140210. Accessed July 17, 2014.

12. Shailagh Murray, "For a Senate Foe of Pork Barrel Politics,
Two Bridges Too Far," *Washington Post* (Oct. 21, 2005) http://
www.washingtonpost.com/wp-dyn/content/article/2005/10/20
/AR2005102001931.html. Accessed July 8, 2014.

13. Author's telephone interview with Senator Tom Coburn, May
4, 2013.

14. Alexander Bolton and Bob Cusack, "Reid: Obamacare Will Help
Dems Hold the Senate Majority in 2014," *The Hill* (Dec. 18, 2013); "His
[Reid's] hallmark as leader has been to strictly limit votes on politically
charged amendments, which Republicans offer to collect political ammo
for Senate campaigns."

15. Mau Raju, "McConnell Blows Up at Harry Reid over Filibuster
Rules," *Politico* (July 18, 2012) http://www.politico.com/news/stories
/0712/78665.html. Accessed July 8, 2014.

16. "Inhofe Joins with Democrats on Quick Defense Authorization
Bill Passage," *The Hill* (Dec. 15, 2013) Thehill.com/blogs/defcon-hill
/budget-appropriations/193153-inhofe-joins-with-dems-on-quick
-defense-bill-passage. Accessed July 8, 2014.

17. Ibid.

18. Ibid.

19. Ibid.

20. Author's telephone interview with Senator Tom Coburn, May
4, 2013.

Chapter 5

1. John Berlau and David Bier, "The Problems with the
STOCK Act," *National Review Online* (Feb. 14, 2012) http://www

.nationalreview.com/articles/290847/problems-stock-act-john-berlau; and "Obama Signs STOCK Act into Law," Associated Press (April 4, 2012) http://www.huffingtonpost.com/2012/04/04/obama-signs -stock-act_n_1402669.html. Both accessed July 8, 2014.

2. "Senate Drops Vote to Penalize Ex-members Who Become Lobbyists," *The Hill* (Feb. 3, 2012) http://thehill.com/blogs/floor-action /senate/208449-senate-wont-vote-on-lifetime-lobbying-ban-. Accessed July 8, 2014.

3. Zachary A. Goldfarb, "JOBS Act: White House, Democrats at Odds over Obama-Backed Pro-business Bill," *Washington Post* (March 26, 2012) http://www.washingtonpost.com/business/economy /jobs-act-white-house-democrats-at-odds-over-pro-business-bill-set-to -pass/2012/03/26/gIQAfnq3cS_story.html. Accessed July 8, 2014.

4. Zach Carter and Ryan Grim, "Obama JOBS Act Leaves Labor Fuming in Democratic Feud," *Huffington Post* (May 20, 2012) http://www.huffingtonpost.com/2012/04/05/obama-jobs-act-labor _n_1404401.html. Accessed July 8, 2014.

5. Author's telephone interview with Senate staff member, Jan. 7, 2014.

6. Mike Elk, "Trumka 'Personally Outraged' by Obama-Backed JOBS Act," *In These Times* (April 11, 2012) http://inthesetimes.com /working/entry/13017/trumka_personally_outraged_by_obama -backed_jobs_act. Accessed July 8, 2014.

7. Goldfarb, "JOBS Act."

8. Notes by the author, March 23, 2012.

9. Deirdre Walsh and Dana Bash, "Congressional Insider Trading Ban Might Not Apply to Families," CNN (July 19, 2012) http:/www.cnn .com/2012/07/19/politics/stock-act-loophole/index.html. Accessed July 8, 2014.

10. Ibid.

11. Joe Davidson, "Heavy Hitters Strike at Stock Act Employee Provisions," *Washington Post* (July 26, 2012) http://www.washingtonpost .com/politics/heavy-hitters-strike-at-stock-act-employee-provisions /2012/07/26/gJQAYBPNCX_story.html. Accessed July 8, 2014.

12. Ibid.

13. Seung Min Kim, "Congress Passes Quick Fix to STOCK Act," *Politico* (Sept. 28, 2012) http://www.politico.com/blogs/on-congress /2012/09/congress-passes-quick-fix-to-stock-act-136932.html. Accessed July 8, 2014.

14. Ibid.

15. http://www.napawash.org.

16. Niels Lesniewski, "STOCK Act Endangers National Security, Report Says," *Roll Call* (March 28, 2013) http://www.rollcall.com /news/stock_act_endangers_national_security_report_says-223494-1 .html. Accessed July 8, 2014.

17. aguadito, "Pres Obama Signs Bill Killing Anti-Corruption, Pro-Transparency STOCK Act Provisions," *Daily Kos* (April 16, 2013) http://www.dailykos.com/story/2013/04/16/1202123/-Obama -Signs-Bill-Killing-Anti-Corruption-Pro-Transparency-STOCK-Act -Provisions. Accessed July 8, 2014.

18. Daniel Horowitz, "The Stock Act: A Look into Drive-By Lawmaking," *RedState* (April 17, 2013) http://www.redstate.com /diary/dhorowitz3/2013/04/17/the-stock-act-a-look-into-drive-by -lawmaking/. Accessed July 8, 2014.

19. Author's telephone interview with Congressional staff member, Jan. 7, 2014, and email exchange, Jan. 14, 2014. This Senate staff member was told by SEC staff that, in the opinion of that agency, it considered insider trading and the use of inside information to influence securities trading by members of Congress to be illegal as of the time that the STOCK Act originally passed Congress.

20. Matt Taibbi, "Why Obama's JOBS Act Couldn't Suck Worse," *Rolling Stone* (April 9, 2012) http://www.rollingstone.com/politics /blogs/taibblog/why-obamas-jobs-act-couldnt-suck-worse-20120409. Accessed July 8, 2014.

21. "How to Harm Investors," *New York Times* (March 29, 2014) http://www.nytimes.com/2014/03/30/opinion/sunday/how-to-harm -investors.html. Accessed July 8, 2014.

Chapter 6

1. Aaron Blake, "Kevin McCarthy's Strange, New Definition of 'Bipartisanship'," *Washington Post* (Sept. 20, 2013) http://www .washingtonpost.com/blogs/the-fix/wp/2013/09/20/kevin-mccarthys -strange-new-definition-of-bipartisan/. Accessed July 8, 2014.

2. See: Lori Montgomery, "Senate Passes Bipartisan Budget Agreement," *Washington Post* (Dec. 18, 2013) http://www .washingtonpost.com/politics/senate-poised-to-pass-bipartisan-budget -agreement/2013/12/18/54fd3a1a-6807-11e3-a0b9-249bbb34602c _story.html; "Senate Passes Bipartisan Budget Agreement," ABC News (Dec. 18, 2013) http://abcnews.go.com/blogs/politics2013

/12/senate-passes-bipartisan-budget-agreement; "Senate Passes Bipartisan Budget Deal," Education Votes (Dec. 18, 2013) http://educationvotes.nea.org/2013/12/18/senate-passes-bipartisan-budget-deal/; Mark Memmott, "Bipartisan Budget Deal Passes Key Test In Senate," NPR (Dec. 17, 2013) http://www.npr.org/blogs/thetwo-way/2013/12/17/251923760/its-looking-like-the-senate-will-approve-the-budget-deal; and Patrick Martin, "US Senate Approves Bipartisan Austerity Budget," World Socialist Web Site (Dec. 19, 2013) http://www.wsws.org/en/articles/2013/12/19/budg-d19html. All accessed July 8, 2014.

3. Carl Hulse, "In Passage of Jobs Measure, a Glimpse of Bipartisanship," *New York Times* (Feb. 22, 2010) http://www.nytimes.com/2010/02/23/us/politics/23jobs.html. Accessed July 8, 2014.

4. See Ben Pershing, "Senate Advances Job-Creation Bill with GOP Help," *Washington Post* (Feb. 23, 2010) http://www.washingtonpost.com/wp-dyn/content/article/2010/02/22/AR2010022204804.html. Accessed July 8, 2014.

5. "Breakaway Republicans Help Move Jobs Bill," CBS News (Feb. 23, 2010) http://www.cbsnews.com/news/breakaway-republicans-help-move-jobs-bill/. Accessed July 29, 2014.

6. Katrina vanden Heuvel, "The Promise of Transpartisanship," *Washington Post* (Jan. 27, 2014) http://www.washingtonpost.com/opinions/katrina-vanden-heuvel-the-promise-of-transpartisanship/2014/01/27/09830c00-877d-11e3-916e-e01534b1e132_story.html. Accessed July 8, 2014.

7. Matt Apuzzo, "Holder and Republicans Unite to Soften Sentencing Laws," *New York Times* (March 3, 2014) http://www.nytimes.com/2014/03/04/us/politics/holder-and-republicans-unite-to-soften-sentencing-laws.html. Accessed July 8, 2014.

8. Laurel Harbridge, Neil Malhotra, and Brian F. Harrison, "Compromise vs. Compromises: Preferences for Bipartisanship in the American Electorate," Paper presented at the 2012 Annual Meeting of the American Political Science Association, p. 3.

9. Ibid., 4.

10. Ibid., 27.

11. "Does Bipartisanship Matter?" *New York Times* (Feb. 23, 2009) http://roomfordebate.blogs.nytimes.com/2009/02/23/does-bipartisanship-matter/?_php=true&_type=blogs&_r=0. Accessed July 8, 2014.

12. Ibid.

13. Ruth Marcus, "Bipartisanship Caving on Military Pension Cut," *Washington Post* (Feb. 11, 2014) http://www.washingtonpost .com/opinions/ruth-marcus-bipartisan-caving-on-military-pension-cut /2014/02/11/3a84561e-9368-11e3-84e1-27626c5ef5fb_story.html. Accessed July 8, 2014.

14. *Economist*, "What Is 'Bipartisanship'?" (Dec. 16, 2010) http:// www.economist.com/node/21014021. Accessed July 8, 2014.

15. Ibid.

16. Mark Mazzetti, "Senators Clear Path for Release of Detention Report on C.I.A.," *New York Times* (April 2, 2014) http://www .nytimes.com/2014/04/03/us/politics/2-senators-clear-way-for -release-of-report-on-cia-detentions.html; Ed O'Keefe, "How Susan Collins Became the Senate's Key Deal-Maker" *Washington Post* (April 3, 2014) http://www.washingtonpost.com/blogs/the-fix/wp /2014/04/03/susan-collins-is-the-most-important-senator-youve -never-heard-of/; and Liz Halloran, "Who's Who in Senate-CIA Report Showdown," NPR (April 3, 2014) http://www.npr.org/blogs /itsallpolitics/2014/04/03/298764174/whos-who-in-senate-cia -report-showdown. Accessed July 8, 2014.

17. Kevin D. Williamson, "Extremism Is Not the Problem; Bipartisanship Is," *National Review* (April 30, 2012) http://www .nationalreview.com/exchequer/297351/extremism-not-problem -bipartisanship. Accessed July 29, 2014.

18. Thomas Frank, "Bipartisanship is a Silly Beltway Obsession," *Wall Street Journal* (Feb. 18, 2009) http://online.wsj.com/news /articles/SB123491659161904365. Accessed July 29, 2014.

19. Matt Purple, "Enough with the Bipartisanship," *American Spectator* (March 24, 2013) http://spectator.org/articles/55533 /enough-bipartisanship. Accessed July 8, 2014.

20. Ibid.

21. "Junk Food in Schools Enjoys Bipartisan Support," Center for Science in the Public Interest (May 20, 2004) https://www.cspinet.org /new/200405201.html. Accessed July 8, 2014.

22. Ibid.

23. FarmPolicy.com, http://farmpolicy.com/2014/02/05/2014 -farm-bill-a-timeline. Accessed July 8, 2014.

24. Dave Juday, "Meet the New Farm Bill," *Weekly Standard* (Feb. 24, 2014) http://www.weeklystandard.com/articles/meet-new -farm-bill_781555.html; and Ed O' Keefe, "Farm Bill Passes in House, without Food Stamp Funding," *Washington Post* (July 11, 2013) http://

www.washingtonpost.com/blogs/post-politics/wp/2013/07/11
/house-republicans-drop-food-stamps-from-new-farm-bill/. Both
accessed July 8, 2014.

25. A quote attributed to Charles Chamberlain, political director
of Democracy for America, in Stephen Dinan, "Bipartisanship in Congress: Good or Bad?" *Washington Times* (March 1, 2010) http://www
.washingtontimes.com/news/2010/mar/01/b-word-stymies-both
-sides-of-the-aisle/?page=all. Accessed July 8, 2014.

26. Quoted in Purple, "Enough with the Bipartisanship."

27. Burgess Everett, "Senators Introduce Bipartisan Ukraine
Resolution," *Politico* (March 5, 2014) http://www.politico.com/story
/2014/03/ukraine-senate-bipartisan-resolution-104306.html. Accessed
July 8, 2014.

28. Ed O'Keefe, "Breaking: Congress Actually Did Its Job This
Week," *Washington Post* (March 14, 2014) http://www.washingtonpost
.com/blogs/the-fix/wp/201403/14/this-week-congress-actually-did
-its-job. Accessed July 8, 2014.

29. "Isakson Praises Senate Passage of Legislation to Protect Homeowners from Flood Insurance Rate Spike," website of US Senator Johnny
Isakson (March 13, 2014) http://www.isakson.senate.gov/public/index
.cfm/2014/3/isakson-praises-senate-passage-of-legislation-to-protect
-homeowners-from-flood-insurance-rate-spike. Accessed July 28, 2014.

30. Andrew G. Simpson, "Senate Approves Bill to Curb Flood Insurance," *Insurance Journal* (March 13, 2014) http://www.insurancejournal
.com/news/national/2014/03/13/323273.htm. Accessed July 8, 2014.

31. Ed O'Keefe and Paul Kane, "Chuck Schumer, Lamar Alexander Might Have Solution to Fixing Senate," *Washington Post* (March
10, 2014) http://www.washingtonpost.com/politics/chuck-schumer
-lamar-alexander-might-have-solution-to-fixing-senate/2014/03/10
/d1635fd6-a302-11e3-a5fa-55f0c77bf39c story.html. Accessed July
8, 2014.

32. Ibid.

33. Author's telephone interview with senator John Boozman, May
9, 2013.

34. Ed O'Keefe, "Senators Reach Bipartisan Deal on a Bill to Fix
VA," *Washington Post* (June 5, 2014) http://www.washingtonpost.com
/blogs/post-politics/wp/2014/06/05/senators-reach-bipartisan-deal
-on-bill-to-fix-va/. Accessed July 8, 2014.

35. See: Sean Theriault, *The Gingrich Senators: The Roots of Partisan
Warfare in Congress* (New York: Oxford University Press, 2013).

36. Author's telephone interview with Senator Mike Crapo, Dec. 21, 2012.

37. Burgess Everett and Darren Goode, "Senate Leaders Give Floor Time to Vulnerable Dems," *Politico* (April 6, 2014) http://www.politico .com/story/2014/04/senate-leaders-give-floor-time-to-vulnerable -dems-105409.html. Accessed July 8, 2014.

38. Scott Horsley, "Tea Party Candidate Uses Immigration to Beat Cantor," NPR, *Morning Edition* (June 12, 2014). http:// www.npr.org/2014/06/12/321218307/tea-party-candidate-uses -immigration-issue-to-beat-cantor. Accessed July 8, 2014.

39. Martin Matishak and Ramsey Cox, "Senate Passes Overhaul of VA in 93-3 Vote," *The Hill* (June 11, 2014) http://thehill.com/blogs /floor-action/senate/209046-senate-passes-va-overhaul. Accessed July 8, 2014.

INDEX

About the Author

Ross K. Baker is distinguished professor of political science at Rutgers University.

Baker, a nationally recognized authority on the US Congress, was a research associate at the Brookings Institution in Washington, DC, before coming to Rutgers in 1968. He obtained both his BA and his PhD from the University of Pennsylvania. Baker is featured on NPR's *All Things Considered*. He is on the board of contributors of *USA Today*, and his commentaries have appeared in the *New York Times*, the *Washington Post*, *Chicago Tribune*, the *Boston Globe*, and the *Philadelphia Inquirer*.

On successive sabbatical leaves starting in 1975, Baker served on the staffs of Senators Walter F. Mondale, Birch Bayh, and Frank Church; as a consultant to the Democratic Caucus of the US House of Representatives in 1982–1983; and as a senior adviser to Senator Chuck Hagel in 2000 (R-NE) and to Patrick J. Leahy in 2004 (D-VT). Most recently (2008 and 2012) Baker was scholar-in-residence in the office of Senate Majority Leader Harry Reid (D-NV), including during the lame-duck session. In 1992, Baker was a Fulbright Fellow at the Swedish Institute of International Affairs in Stockholm.

His books include *The Afro-American* (Van Nostrand, 1970), *Friend and Foe in the U.S. Senate* (The Free Press, 1980, and Copley, 1999), *The New Fat Cats* (Priority Press, 1989), and *House and Senate* (W. W. Norton, 1989, 1995, 2000, and 2008). He also coauthored *American Government* (1983 and 1987).